Acknowledgements

KU-592-637

We wish to thank the following for providing the ideas behind a number of activities in this book.

Cynthia Beresford for *Shields* (Activity 52)
Vanessa Burke for *Spell it write* (Activity 45)
Charles Cummins for *Student worksheets* (Activity 56)
David Eastment and Janet Raynor for *Treasure hunt* (Activity 14)
Charlie Farrell for *Famous writers* (Activity 87)
Louise Finlayson for *If I ruled the world* (Activity 15)
David Forbes and Robert Gizzi for the worksheets for *Presents for all* (Activity 20)
Louis Gillespie for *Reading about London* (Activity 31)
Peter Goode and Paul Seligson for *Book reviews* (Activity 54)
Peter McCreadie for *Sound me out* (Activity 44)
John Morgan and Mario Rinvolucri for *Five in one story* (Activity 41)
Anita Pincas for *The American tourist* (Activity 42)
Joseph Rezeau for *Personal letters* (Activity 36)

To Antónia and Sandra

Contents

2.3 Word focus

2.4 Learner training focus

The authors and series editor

David Hardisty worked in the United Kingdom with Indo-Chinese refugees after graduating in Peace Studies. He then worked in Sudan, teaching Sudanese nationals and Eritrean refugees. After taking a postgraduate certificate in education in English to Speakers of Other Languages he went to Portugal where he worked for the British Council developing and coordinating facilities for Computer Assisted Language Learning. His other contributions to CALL have been helping to run teacher training courses at Lancaster University and giving a number of talks and workshops at international conferences. He has also published articles on CALL and a variety of ELT subjects.

Scott Windeatt has taught in Finland, Rumania and Austria. His subject areas have included English as a Foreign Language, English for Specific Purposes, Teacher training and Applied Linguistics. He has also taught Modern Languages in comprehensive schools in Britain. He has worked at the Institute for English Language Education at the University of Lancaster since 1979. His interests include CALL, self-access learning, the teaching of grammar, and language testing. He has co-authored with Ann Brumfit on *Communicative Grammar* — a series of books with problem-solving exercises. He has also written many articles.

Alan Maley worked for The British Council from 1962–1988, serving as English Language Officer in Yugoslavia, Ghana, Italy, France, and China, and as Regional Representative for The British Council in South India (Madras). He is currently Director-General of the Bell Educational Trust, Cambridge.

He wrote *Quartet* (with Françoise Grellet and Wim Welsing, OUP, 1982) and *Literature* also in this series (with Alan Duff, OUP 1990). He has also written *Beyond Words, Sounds Interesting, Sounds Intriguing, Words, Variations on a Theme*, and *Drama Techniques in Language Learning* (all with Alan Duff), *The Mind's Eye* (with Françoise Grellet and Alan Duff), and *Learning to Listen and Poem into Poem* (with Sandra Moulding). He is also Series Editor for the New Perspectives and Oxford Supplementary Skills series.

Foreword

Computer Assisted Language Learning (CALL) is the latest in the series of modern aids to language learning which began with the gramophone. One problem with these new devices has been that each has tended to generate a wave of euphoria, rapidly followed by a trough of frustration and disillusionment. Although teachers still tend to look for miracle methods, their experience with, for example, language laboratories, has taught them to be wary of the benefits of technology and to appraise each new advance with a critical eye. This new realism is a welcome sign of maturity.

Another positive development is the closing of the time-gap between the introduction of new technology and finding appropriate applications for it. It took the profession fifteen or more years to find effective ways of utilizing language laboratories. It has taken CALL a considerably shorter time to move from its crude beginnings ('space-age technology to purvey stone-age methodology') to a stage where the use of computers is both innovative and truly appropriate.

So CALL is here to stay. No one who has observed the atmosphere of total absorption of a group of students using computers can doubt its motivational power. And the range and sophistication of its applications is increasing with extraordinary rapidity.

Unfortunately, the idea of using computers strikes fear and dread into the hearts of the uninitiated. This book offers a relatively gentle introduction to the field. It is an impressive attempt to present a complex and rapidly changing scene in a comprehensible and accessible way.

The authors are at pains to point out that CALL is not a universal panacea but simply another medium, albeit a powerful one, for promoting learning. With time CALL will come to be taken for granted in much the same way as are OHPs or tape-recorders. This book moves us several steps towards that happy day.

Alan Maley

Introduction

What is CALL?

CALL stands for Computer Assisted Language Learning. It is the term most commonly used by teachers and students to describe the use of computers as part of a language course. It does not refer to the use of a computer by a teacher to type out a worksheet, or by an educational institution to provide a computerized bill for a student for language course fees.

Other terms used in this book include:

Hardware — this refers to any computer equipment used, including the computer itself, the keyboard, the screen (or monitor), the disc-drive and the printer.

Software (or programs) — this refers to the sets of instructions which need to be loaded into the computer for it to be able to work.

What do you need to know to use this book?

This book is intended as an introduction to computer-assisted language learning, rather than to computers. We assume that the reader, or someone in the reader's class or institution:

1 can switch a computer system on;
2 is familiar with a computer keyboard;
3 can load a program into the computer (e.g. from a disc);
4 can start the program working.

Appendix E provides some technical details about computer equipment. Otherwise, if you are not clear about any of these points, check with your computer manuals, your computer dealer, or the person in your institution assigned to managing the computers.

What equipment do you need?

1 What sort of computers do you need?

We are very conscious that this book will be read by users of many different types of computer, and so we have tried to include only activities which use software available for a variety of common machines or operating systems. If you are thinking of buying a computer, it is important to check that it will run the software you want to use. If there is no, or very little, CALL software available for it, check that it at least has some good applications software such as word-processing, databases and spreadsheets available for it (see Chapter 1).

Appendix F offers advice on how you can obtain software for a variety of machines.

2 How many machines do you need?

Every activity indicates how many machines will be needed to carry it out. Normally, this book assumes that one computer will be available for a group of students. For activities which require all of the students to be able to see the screen, we have found an ideal size of group to be three: with four students round a machine, the outer two can feel left out of the activity. However, in many teaching situations, there may not be enough machines for such small groups, and the notes at the end of each activity indicate whether it can be carried out with one machine. In addition, Appendix C lists all the activities, indicating whether they can be carried out with just one computer in the class.

Another solution to the problems posed by a lack of machines is to make use of the fact that a typical activity in this book has three stages — pre-computer work, work done at the computer, and post-computer work. It is often possible to organize a lesson so that, while some of the class are working at the computer, the others are doing pre- or post-computer work. Alternatively, two separate activities, one involving CALL and one not, can be planned. The two halves of a class can then do the CALL activity on separate days.

3 Do you need any other equipment?

Each activity lists any other equipment, such as a tape-recorder, which is needed for the activity.

Organizing the equipment

The way in which computers can be used in the language classroom depends not only on the number of machines available, but on the physical organization of the equipment as well. There are four main ways of organizing this.

1 The computer room

The most common way of organizing computers is to locate them in one special purpose computer room. Ideally, there should be separate areas set aside in the room for work at the computers, and for non-computer work. The furniture should also allow group work at machines. A long bench with four computers close together will not allow twelve, and certainly not sixteen students, to use those machines.

2 In the classroom

If you see your main use of CALL as activities involving one computer per class, or activities which use the computer to obtain information (see the section on library programs, Chapter 1), which is then used away from the machine, it may be better to have one computer in each of your classrooms. If it is not possible to leave the computer permanently in the room, a common solution is to install the equipment on a trolley which can be wheeled into the classroom for the lesson.

3 Other locations

Given sufficient resources, some computers should be available for the exclusive use of teachers in a teachers' room. Teachers will then be encouraged to use the computer, especially for word-processing, gaining confidence in their ability to use the equipment in the process.

If possible, computers should also be available in a self-access facility for use by students, who will similarly gain confidence in using the equipment. (If this is the case, it is important to decide exactly what material you will allow students to have access to outside lessons. It can cause problems for teachers if they plan a lesson around a piece of software that some of the students have already worked through on their own.)

Finally, it is useful to have one computer with a large screen functioning as an electronic noticeboard for messages prepared by students and staff. This should be located in a public part of the institution, such as the entrance hall or library.

4 Network, or stand-alone?

A computer by itself is called a stand-alone machine. Computers that are linked together so that they can use each other's material and send each other information and messages, are said to form a Local Area Network (or LAN for short).

A few of the lessons in this book require a Local Area Network. Running a network is more difficult than managing stand-alone machines, and in educational institutions that have them, a network manager looks after the system. One advantage is that the teachers and students usually then need to know very little about the system in order to use it. Another is that, in a language classroom oriented around communicative activities, the ability of a computer to communicate with other computers is particularly useful. We would suggest that institutions use a Network if they have someone who can act as Network Manager.

5 Which is the best way of organizing the equipment?

In an ideal world an institution would have enough money to install computers in all of these locations, linked together as a Network, but still able to function by themselves if the Network breaks down.

Most teachers have less than ideal conditions – and often have decisions about equipment purchases taken out of their hands. If you can influence these decisions, however, try to decide what sort of organization would be most useful for CALL (rather than, for example, computer studies or information technology classes). In particular, if you are going to have just one computer available, try to get a screen big enough for all your students to see (or a display device which will allow you to project the picture from the computer onto an overhead projector).

Is there a special CALL methodology?

The most important point to make is that computers are not very good at teaching by themselves. How effective computers are in the language classroom will therefore depend on the way the teacher and students use them, and in this respect they are no different from any other medium. Computers are, however, different from other media in two main respects. They can allow the user to:

1 carry out tasks which are impossible in other media (such as automatically providing feedback on certain kinds of exercise);

2 carry out tasks much more conveniently than in other media (such as editing a piece of writing by deleting, moving and inserting text).

The main effect that these features have on methodology is that students can:

3 work through some exercises on their own and have them marked automatically by the computer (multiple-choice and total-deletion programs provide examples of this);

4 carry out exploratory work which is not assessed by the computer, but which allows them to see the results of their decisions (word-processing, spreadsheet and simulation programs provide examples of this).

Students will usually gain more from these activities, however, if there is an opportunity for them to discuss with the teacher the work they have done on the computer. For that reason the methodology adopted in the lessons in this book is similar to that which we would adopt in a non-CALL class. The main characteristics of that methodology are:

1 The use of a variety of interaction patterns in class

Figure 1a below suggests the variety of interaction patterns which are possible with computers. Students can work individually, in pairs and groups, or as a whole class. Each student within each group can be assigned different roles, and each group can interact in various ways with the computer, the other groups and the teacher.

When considering the activities in this book, it is useful to ask the following questions:

— *What have the students been doing?*
— *What has the teacher been doing?*
— *What has the computer been doing?*

In one CALL lesson we gave, the answers to these questions were as follows:

Students
writing/editing/commenting/reading others' work/asking for help/learning terminology/talking to each other/operating computers/listening to and implementing instructions/laughing (a lot)/

Teacher
guiding/explaining/editing/keeping control/reassuring and encouraging/doing other class work/giving instructions/observing/correcting/

Computer
memorizing/storing/providing a stimulus/moving and transferring information/saving time/anonymous editing/printing/

Of course, these will vary from activity to activity — in some, the teacher will need to be a facilitator, in others a leader, and in some the teacher will be free to give more individual attention to students who particularly need this attention. (See Fig. 1b.) We suggest that when you try CALL activities out, you make lists from your own observations.

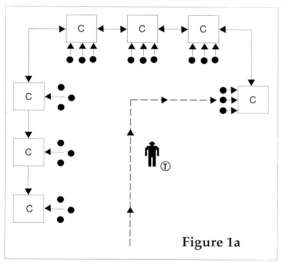

Figure 1a

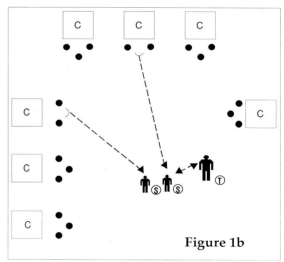

Figure 1b

2 Information-transfer and information- and opinion-gap tasks

Information-transfer
Many of our activities involve transferring information from one medium to another, from student to student, or from group to group. Students listen to a tape-recording of a story and then sequence the events of the story, or match sentences spoken with the characters in a story, or load a text written by another group of students into a word-processor. One of the main reasons for suggesting the use of networked computers is that this provides the optimum conditions for information-transfer activities.

Information-gap
Our lessons frequently involve an information-gap, with one student, or group of students needing information from others in

the class to complete an activity. Sometimes the computer itself has the information: programs involving total or partial deletion (see Chapter 1) are examples of activities based on such an information gap.

Opinion-gap
A number of our lessons are based on opinion-gap activities. The students involved will have different opinions concerning a problem-solving scenario, such as the cheapest way of allocating resources in a spreadsheet, or a simulation, or the best way out of a maze in an adventure. Alternatively, the difference of opinion may be over the best ending to a short story written on a word-processor. Assigning different roles to students ('You are in favour of X', or 'You are in favour of Y'), can be important in maintaining a creative opinion-gap.

3 Fluency and accuracy practice

One of the features of many CALL programs is that the students have to type in exactly the answer the computer expects, since the computer can only accept the answers it has been programmed to accept. This limitation can in practice be very useful, since it provides a motivation for the student to use the language as accurately as possible. Programs such as word-processing, however, can be used for both accuracy and fluency practice, and pre- and post-computer work with any program can focus on both aspects.

4 Computer-work, pre-computer work and post-computer work

In our activities, there are always three stages — pre-computer work before the students use the machines—work done at the computer—and post-computer work done away from the computers. In some cases, the actual period spent at the computer may be very limited. For example, in many simulations the students need only go to the computer to type in their decisions. Any discussion can take place away from the computer.

Are there any 'rules' to follow when using computers?

There are no hard and fast rules, but the following guidelines will be useful:

1 The software is more important than the hardware. Don't worry too much about the type of computer you have, provided it will run the sort of programs you want to use. It is more important to be able to use a variety of useful software.

2 Get to know the software. It can take longer to get to know a piece of CALL software well than it can a textbook, because you have to work your way through it, rather than just skimming through it. But it is worth spending the time.

3 Software varies in its complexity. It is possible to learn how to use a typical 'Total Deletion' program in a few minutes. The basics of word-processing can be learnt in half an hour (though it can take months to fully understand all the facilities of a powerful word-processor). Most language teachers find word-processors easier to learn than, for example, databases.

4 'Any teacher who can be replaced by a computer should be.' (Anon). Computers aren't very good at teaching by themselves, and the software won't run your lessons for you. You can adapt, improve and compensate for shortcomings in the software with the techniques you adopt. (You can also misuse the software!)

5 Co-operate with your students. They may well know more than you do about computers, so you can exchange your knowledge about language and teaching for their experience of using the equipment.

6 Don't panic! If things go wrong, most of the time there will be a simple solution (Have you switched all of the equipment on?).

How to use this book

This book has been designed with two kinds of reader in mind. Firstly, the reader who already has experience in using computers and is dipping into the book to pick up more ideas. Secondly, the reader who is still quite new to Computer Assisted Language Learning, who may have learnt the basics of switching a computer on, and putting a disc into a disc-drive, but is still rather unsure about the educational possibilities of this technology.

There are a number of ways in which this book can be used:

1 If you are new to CALL concentrate on becoming familiar with the types of program which are available. Read about a particular type of software in Chapter 1, then investigate some of the activities in Chapter 2 which use the same software. To find the relevant activities, use the list at the front of the book, and Appendix A. 'Total deletion' software is a good program type to start with, as it is straightforward to use, and usually popular with students.

2 Those with a little more experience of CALL may also prefer to work through the book systematically, treating it as an instruction manual. We would suggest that the first time you read through the book in this way you miss out any parts which you find complex, and save them for a second reading.

3 A third way to use this book, especially for more experienced CALL users, is simply to dip into it for activities which you find interesting, or which would be suitable for a course you are teaching. We would suggest that you dip into Chapters 2 and 3 but read the explanation in Chapter 1 of any program type you are not familiar with.

4 Experienced users of CALL could look at activities using software they are less familiar with. They could also concentrate on adapting activities to suit their particular teaching situation. In addition, they might work through one of the schemes of work in Chapter 3 and then develop a scheme of work of their own.

Chapter organization

In order to help different kinds of reader the book is divided into three Chapters.

Chapter 1 — Program types

This is an introduction to the types of software which have been used in this book. We have deliberately chosen programs or program types which exist for most standard computers. These are grouped into sections on programs developed originally for school, office, library and home.

A description of the program is given, which indicates what computer knowledge is needed to use it. A straightforward sample activity is then given which can be used to help the reader to build up confidence in using the program.

Chapter 2 — Activities

This chapter contains a bank of ideas for the use of computers in the classroom. These activities are organized into those which provide practice in syntax, skills, lexis and learner training.

Chapter 3 — Schemes of work

This chapter consists of schemes of work, which are a series of lessons showing how CALL can be integrated into the general curriculum of a language course. Examples are included for a range of types of learner — beginners, examination candidates, advanced students and pre-undergraduate students.

Appendices

Several appendices provide different ways of accessing the material in the book. They provide information on:

A Activities grouped according to program type
B Activities grouped according to linguistic level
C Activities for use with one computer in a classroom, for self-access and for users with varying degrees of experience of CALL
D Useful contact addresses
E Buying computer equipment
F Published software

How the activities are organized

The description for each activity contains the following information:

Aim
The objective of the activity

Level
The level of learner with which the activity can be carried out

Time
An indication of the time the activity is likely to take

Preparation
This section indicates what the teacher should prepare before the lesson. It is divided into:

Hardware
The equipment needed, including non-computer hardware such as
a tape-recorder

Software
The type of software used

Knowledge needed
What the teachers and the students need to be able to do with the
computer and the software in order to carry out the activity

Procedure
This is divided into:

Pre-computer work
The work done before the students sit in front of a screen

Computer work
The parts of the activity carried out at the keyboard

Post-computer work
Follow-up activities

Notes
These include suggestions for modifying the activities for use:

1 With different levels of learner
2 With different amounts of hardware, including one computer in
  a class
3 With different software

1 Program types

Introduction

We have used many different programs in our lessons. Most of these are available in a similar form – though not necessarily with the same name – for other computers than the ones we have been using, and a number of the programs we have used, although they have different names, are in fact very similar to each other. That is why we have set out in this chapter not to describe *all* of the programs that figure in our lessons plans, but to describe the different program *types* we have used. In that way, even if you do not have the exact program we refer to in a particular lesson, you should be able to use our description of the program type to which it belongs to identify whether you have a similar program, or to find out if one is available for your own computer.

As well as describing the main features of the different types of program, we have included comments based on our own experience of using them in the classroom, and a description of at least one lesson which we have taught using each program type. The main characteristic of these lesson plans is that you should be able to use them even if you are unfamiliar with the technology and the programs. This sometimes means that the lessons do not show the full potential of a program. Once you feel more confident, however, you should then look at the other suggestions for using the programs, in Chapters 2 and 3.

One characteristic of the programs we have used – and one which we think is of great importance – is that most of them have authoring facilities, whereby teachers (and students, for some activities) type in their own texts or questions, and sometimes clues or explanations. This allows for different levels, interests, and topics. Many of our lessons depend on this facility being available.

Chapter organization

The different kinds of software have been divided into sections labelled with a particular 'location', as follows:

Label	Role	Category	Description
'School'	teacher	exercises	cognisant
'Office'	worker	applications	assistant
'Library'	librarian	page turning	informant
'Home'	family	entertaining	stimulant

We start in the 'school' with programs which mirror common exercises in a language institution — gap-filling, multiple-choice questions, sequencing and matching exercises. The section finishes with an exercise type created by CALL for the language institution — total-deletion.

The school is followed by the 'office' and the programs frequently used there — word-processors, databases, desktop publishing/ graphics programs, communications software, and spreadsheets.

The next location is the 'library' which contains programs that supply information—viewdata and concordancing programs.

Finally, we return 'home', utilizing two program types frequently used in the home for entertainment — simulations and adventures.

Use of the chapter

You should expect to find some software which you find particularly useful, and other software which is useless in your opinion.

For activities which you like, see if they share any common elements. Look particularly at ways that get the learners interacting with (a) each other and (b) the computer. Look also at the factors which lead to student (non) involvement in the activity. Write down what the teacher, the computer, and the students do.

Use these answers and the notes on suggestions for modifications to the activity and see if you can build up a bank of CALL activities.

1.1 'School' programs

The activities shown in this section are:
- Gap-filling
- Multiple-choice
- Sequencing
- Matching
- Total-deletion

SUMMARY OF ACTIVITIES:

Program type	Example activity	Level	Time	Name
Gap-filling	1 Verb parts	E	30 mins	'Verb parts'
Multiple-choice	2 Spelling	I	20–45 mins	'It's all Greek to me'
Sequencing	3 Question forms	B	55 mins	'Question check'
Matching	4 Literature	A	45 mins	'Toby or not toby'
Total-deletion	5 Inviting	E	30–60 mins	'Invitations'

Gap-filling

Gap-filling exercises are one of the most common activities found in language-learning textbooks, and there are many computerized versions available. (These are sometimes known as partial-deletion, or partial-reconstruction programs.)

The main features which can be found in such programs (though it is unlikely that any one program will have all of them) are as follows:

1 Length of text

Programs vary in the length of text which they allow in each exercise. Some allow connected texts of 100–300 words (up to three screenfuls of connected text); others allow a number of questions in an exercise, but only three or four lines (perhaps 20 words) per question; some allow either.

2 Items to be gapped

Programs may allow letters, single words, or whole phrases to be gapped.

3 Selection of items to be gapped

Some programs allow words to be deleted only at fixed intervals (for example, every fifth, seventh, or twelfth word). Other programs allow the user to select exactly which words are to be deleted.

4 Help given to the student

Students may simply be told if their selected answer is right or wrong. Some programs allow clues to be given, and some explanations as well.

5 Flexibility

Some programs can be used only as tests, allowing the student a fixed number of tries at completing a gap (either one or two is the most common number). Others allow the student to use the program either as a test, or as a tutorial (in which case the student can have as many tries at an answer as he or she wishes, and may be able to call up clues and explanations), or even in an exploratory mode (where students have more than one correct answer available to be discovered).

Although some versions are easier to use than others, the exercise-type is so familiar that students and teachers are unlikely to find much difficulty in using gap-filling programs. Because of the familiarity of the exercise-type the teacher can concentrate on learning to use the new technology, while students tend to find the extra degree of interaction that the computer provides over paper-and-pencil exercises motivating, as well as the element of competition involved in trying to 'beat the computer'. The first stage of CALL use is often characterized by such paper-and-pencil like activities, because of their usefulness in building up confidence. We do feel it is important to stress, however, that teachers should not stop at this first stage, but go on to other, more innovative, programs.

Gap-filling or partial-deletion/reconstruction programs are information-gap exercises, and pre-computer activities can provide a framework for the transfer of this unknown information, as in the following example.

1 Verb parts

AIM

To practise irregular verb forms

LEVEL

Elementary

TIME

30 minutes

PREPARATION

Hardware
Preferably one computer per group.

Software
A gap-filling program which can be authored and which allows the user to choose which words are blanked out.

Knowledge
Teacher — authoring the program. Students — using the program.

PROCEDURE

Pre-computer work:

1 Give students a list of irregular verbs which you wish to practise or revise. The students work in pairs, and there should be one copy of the list for each pair.

2 One student has the list (to test his/her partner). They have three minutes to find and note down as many mistakes as they can.

3 Students change roles.

4 The teacher checks which verbs caused problems.

Computer-work:

5 Students are given a table of the irregular verbs on screen, with various parts blanked out. Students must reconstruct the blanks.

Post-computer work:

6 Students have to choose five of the verbs and write sentences about the class, some of which are true and some of which are false.

7 Students read or listen to the sentences, trying to spot the false sentences.

MODIFICATIONS

Level
This activity can be used for revision for intermediate students, or even for advanced students with less common irregular verbs.

Hardware

One computer with a large screen could be used with a whole class. A printer would be useful for preparing the lists to be used in the pre-computer activities. The teacher could prepare these using the program and print them out.

Software

A program which deletes words at random (for example, every fifth or seventh word, could be used), but not all of the words which caused students difficulty would be practised.

The activity could also be done on a word-processor, though the teacher or other students would have to indicate if answers were correct.

Procedure

It would be particularly useful to provide a bank of such activities in self-access mode.

Students can do the computer work individually, either by having enough computers for each student, or by allowing each other to go to the computer(s) one by one, while the rest of the class is working on something else.

Alternatively they can work in pairs or groups, competing against the computer, or competing against each other, with students taking turns to fill in the gaps. The activity could even be done with a whole class, with teams competing against each other, and the teacher typing in the answers. The students could author material using the verbs which their colleagues had made mistakes with, in stage 2.

This activity could be integrated with the use of a Network conferencing facility to peer-test irregular verbs, as outlined on page 62.

Comment: This is quite a traditional activity to do on the computer. The computer part is drill-like. There is often a tendency to use drills too much, or not at all, on computer. While other lessons in this book exploit the ability of the computer in more communicative ways, we still feel it is important that CALL users are aware of this possible use of CALL, and make their own decisions on what exercise types to carry out. As will be seen (for example, with the activity on page 98, that is, the pronunciation lesson), a gap-filling program can even be used to reinforce pronunciation.

See Appendix A for more examples of activities using gap-filling programs, and Appendix F for information on gap-filling programs.

Multiple-choice

A number of the program-types described in this chapter may be multiple-choice in one or other of their versions. It is, however, worth describing multiple-choice programs separately, if only because they make use of what is perhaps the most common language-learning exercise to be found in any medium.

Multiple-choice exercises on the computer typically come in two basic forms. The most familiar consists of a body of text followed by multiple-choice alternatives, for example:

> This is a sentence which begins with the word . . . . . .
> **A** is **B** with **C**. This **D** begins.

The other form, however, is rather more innovative in the way it makes use of the computer's facilities, as the alternatives appear in turn in the sentence itself. The student can therefore evaluate the alternatives in context, before making a final choice, as in the following example:

> This is a sentence which begins with the word *is*. [Press a key]
> This is a sentence which begins with the word *with*. [Press a key]
> This is a sentence which begins with the word *This*. [Press a key]
> This is a sentence which begins with the word *begins*.

Both forms can be used at first to practise conventional multiple-choice material, and also to author it (write your own). In fact the first – the 'traditional' form – is best suited to comprehension questions, and the second to gap-filling exercises. The following example uses the second form of multiple-choice presentation, in which the alternatives are used to create an oral fluency task.

2 It's all Greek to me

AIM
: **To practise spelling words of Greek origin**

LEVEL
: **Intermediate**

TIME
: **20 minutes (45 with variation)**

PREPARATION
: **Hardware**
One computer per group of students.

Software
A multiple-choice program, preferably of the kind which presents the multiple-choice options in context.

Knowledge
Teacher — authoring the program. Students — using (optionally, authoring) the program.

Before the lesson, students should be asked to bring a list of five words which they have spelled wrongly in their written work. The teacher should have authored sentences with words of Greek origin into the program, with favourite spelling mistakes as distractors.

PROCEDURE

Pre-computer work:
1 Ask students to spell *philosophy, psychiatrist.* Point out the problem of 'i' and 'y'.

Computer-work:
2 Students do the multiple-choice exercise, making a note in their books of any words spelled wrongly.

Post-computer work:
3 Students discuss which words they got wrong.

NOTES

This is a straightforward paper-like activity. It is useful, however, in getting students and teachers used to computers, and to writing material with an authoring program.

MODIFICATIONS

Level
Vary the words to be spelled, to raise or lower the level of difficulty.

Hardware
If you have only one computer, you should plan a normal lesson, for example, based on group writing, and get the students to do the computer activity one group at a time.

Software
Many word-processors (see page 30) have a spelling checker, which can be used to check spelling, and even to generate lists of words, for example, those beginning with 'ph'.

Procedure
The activity on page 100 also practises spelling. It is very useful to build up a bank of spelling activities, as the basis for self-access remedial work on spelling.

See Appendix A for more examples of activities using multiple-choice programs, and Appendix F for information on multiple-choice programs.

Sequencing

Another familiar language-learning exercise which has been translated to the computer is sequencing, or re-ordering. A typical exercise would present the student with a jumbled sentence, which he or she would have to restore to its correct order. For example:

the order Put words the correct into

would be reassembled to:

Put the words into the correct order

The main features found in such programs are:

1 Length of text
Sequencing programs most commonly work by jumbling up words in a phrase or sentence, or by jumbling up lines of text on a screen (rather than whole sentences). Some programs do allow sentences or even paragraphs to be jumbled up, but these usually require the teacher to jumble the text, rather than doing this automatically.

2 Help given to the student
Sequencing programs tend to provide few help facilities in the form of either clues or explanations.

This program type is clearly especially suitable for structures which can cause problems of word order, for example, question formation (*Are you going to the cinema tonight?*) or negative adverbs of restriction (*Under no circumstances should you press BREAK*). It is less useful in reordering sentences whose words can be ordered in several ways — for instance, sentences with a lot of adjectives. It is potentially very useful for practising discourse markers (for example, pronouns which refer back to something mentioned in a previous sentence, articles, and expressions setting out a sequence, such as *first, next, then, finally*).

A typical way of using the program is to get a class/group to reorder sentences which are already in the program (perhaps authored by the teacher), then for the students to write their own sentences, preferably with a (perhaps macabre) twist (*Rarely is a murder committed so coldly; Under no circumstances should the body be moved*). Their fellow students in other groups or classes can then use these re-written sentences. This creates a chain: class or group B use class or group A's sentences to practise, then produce sentences of their own for class or group C, and so on.

3 Question check

AIM	**To consolidate work on elementary question formation**
LEVEL	**Beginner**
TIME	**55 minutes**
PREPARATION	**Hardware** One computer per group of students. **Software** A sequencing program. **Knowledge** Teacher — authoring the program. Students — using the program.

Before the lesson, the teacher should type in suitable questions, for example, *What's your name? Where do you live?* etc. These forms should have been presented in previous lessons.

The post-computer work is best done in a classroom which allows students to move around easily.

PROCEDURE

Pre-computer work:
1 Elicit the various question forms.
2 Explain to students how to use the program.

Computer-work:
3 Students put the words of the questions in order and write the questions down in their notebooks.

Post-computer work:
4 Students use the questions that they have constructed, and move round the class, asking and recording answers to the questions.
5 With different students, exchange the information obtained in stage 4.

MODIFICATIONS

Level
With more advanced classes, the exercise can be done as remedial work, using questions which tend to give students particular problems.

Hardware
One computer with a large screen can be used, with the students put into (competing) groups, to see which group unscrambles each sentence first.

Software
A word-processor can also be used instead of a sequencing program, but we feel the interaction of a dedicated program is useful in this lesson.

Procedure
This material can be made available in a self-access facility. The class procedure could be added to by students returning to the computer, after stage 5, and typing the information they have obtained either into a word-processor (see page 30) or a database (see page 35).

See Appendix A for more examples of activities using sequencing programs, and Appendix F for information on sequencing programs.

Matching

Another exercise-type which is commonly found in language-learning textbooks is a matching activity. The learner is presented with two lists of items – which may be single words, phrases, or sentences – and has to match an item in the first list with the relevant item in the second list. Such exercises may, for example, ask the student to match up words which are opposites (*big* in one list, with *small* in the other), or phrases which, together, make a coherent sentence (*The postman* in one list, with *delivered the parcel* in the other). The main features which are found in such programs are:

1 Length of text
Programs may allow lists which consist of single words, phrases, or sentences.

2 Help given to the student
Students may simply be told if their selected match is right or wrong. Some programs allow clues to be given, and some explanations as well.

3 Flexibility
Some programs can be used only as tests, allowing the student a fixed number of tries at finding a match (either one or two is the most common number). Others allow the student to use the program either as a test, or as a tutorial (in which case the student can have as many tries at a match as he or she wishes, and may be able to call up clues and explanations). Less common are those which allow more than one match per item.

4 Supplementary exercises
Some programs come with supplementary exercises, such as a computerized SNAP game in which words from two lists are presented side-by-side on the screen. Only one word from each list is shown at a time, and the words in each list are changed alternately. Students have to press a key if they see a match between the two lists on the screen. Another game which is found is a version of pelmanism, in which students have to remember locations of words on the screen in order to find matching pairs.

As well as being a common language-learning activity, matching is particularly suited to computerization, as the student can physically move the items in each list around the screen in order to see the end-result of his or her choice before making the final selection. This is not possible with such exercises in a book, and only awkwardly possible with scraps of paper. There are, nevertheless, relatively few matching programs available, perhaps because of the difficulty of writing programs which allow text to be manipulated on the screen in the way that is necessary for matching activities. For the CALL user, however, the familiarity of the exercise-type means that matching programs are relatively simple even for newcomers to use.

We have found it useful to have a program which allows for multiple matches. This allows for more creative exercises, though it does mean that you have to be careful when authoring material. It is, of course, possible to use the Move facilities of a word-processor (see page 30) to match words or phrases, though a dedicated program has the advantage of being able to inform the user if the match is right or wrong.

4 Toby or not toby

AIM

To revise the contents of a literary 'set' book

LEVEL

Advanced

TIME

75 minutes

PREPARATION

Hardware
One computer per group of students.

Software
A matching type program.

Knowledge
Teacher — authoring the program. Students — authoring and using the program.

Before the class, the teacher should have authored some material into the program.

PROCEDURE

Pre-computer work:
1 Elicit the story of the novel or play: work on the main scenes.

2 Get students in pairs to produce summaries of the characters: give each group one or two characters (depending on the size of the class and / or cast).

3 Students should tell each other the character profiles they have worked out.

4 Explain to the students that they are going to see a list of characters on one side of the screen, and quotations on the other.

Computer-work:
5 Students match the quotations with the characters.

Post-computer work:
6 Students discuss which quotations were most difficult to identify, and whether this was because the quotations were obscure, or because parts of the text were not well known.

7 Students then author further material for their colleagues, with steps 5 and 6 being repeated.

MODIFICATIONS

Level
The basic exercise can be applied at lower levels, for example, the quotations can come from dialogue phrases in an elementary or intermediate students' textbook. The exercise can be done with

locations, instead of characters: in addition, the quotes can be from different plays or books, by the same author. Alternatively, quotations can be from books of different eras, with the quotations deliberately chosen to bring out archaic language, specific to certain time periods.

Hardware
The activity can be done with one computer and a large screen, especially if the class is reasonably small.

Software
The exercise can also be used with a gap-fill or multiple-choice type program, where the blanks to be filled in are the characters. A bank of such material could be collected for self-access. It would be particularly useful for candidates before an examination.

The activity can also be part of a multi-activity lesson, with students, one group at a time, authoring their own material, for other students to guess, while another activity based on the book is in progress.

For more ideas on exploiting literary texts, see Jean Greenwood's *Class Readers* in this series (OUP 1988).

See Appendix A for more examples of activities using matching programs, and Appendix F for information on matching programs.

Total-deletion

Probably the most common language-learning program available is one which, interestingly enough, is rarely found in a non-computerized form. Total-deletion programs (often called text-reconstruction programs) present the student with a text on the screen in which all of the words have been blanked out. The student is therefore faced with a screen on which the only clues to the content of the text are the title, the punctuation, and (usually) a square or dash to mark each of the letters in the words. The task which the student faces is to re-construct the text by typing in a word he or she thinks the text contains. The program will then search through the text and, if the word occurs anywhere in the text, will insert it in the correct place (or places, if it occurs more than once).

There are an enormous number of examples of such programs, but the main features which are likely to be found in them are:

1 Length of text
Most versions of this program limit the number of words to no more than will fit onto one screen. This may be because of the awkwardness of having to scroll the screen up and down constantly

to check whether the computer has inserted a word in a place in the text which is off the screen. Alternatively, it might be that, given the nature of the exercise, little is to be gained from having a long text.

2 Help given to the student

It would be difficult to provide explanations, or sophisticated clues, since the text is likely to be reconstructed differently each time it is done (which means that it is impossible to predict what words are going to be displayed on the screen when a learner asks for help). Clues are usually limited to showing the first letter of a word, though some programs allow the learner to ask for any letter in a word. Especially useful are programs which allow the student to ask for prefixes or suffixes (so that if the student thinks the text contains some form of the word *dance*, he or she can ask the computer to show him or her where the stem *danc* occurs in the text. He or she can then try the suffixes *es*, *ed*, *ing* and so on. Some programs also record the words which have been tried and in what order, and one or two programs even allow 'replays' of the activity – going through the text and reconstructing it in the order in which the student completed it.

This type of program has proved to be one of the most popular in the initial wave of CALL. One sign of this popularity is the increasing number of versions of it which exist.

Students get very involved in reconstructing the text, and experience a feeling of satisfaction when successfully completing the task. Additionally, the program in fact creates an information gap between itself and the users. It shows the words to be guessed (an essential of an information gap in language teaching is that knowledge of the gap itself must be known).

This information gap can be exploited in a variety of ways. Students can engage in pre-computer activities which help in the reconstruction of the text, and can use the information obtained in the discovered task, to do a follow-up task. Furthermore, the information given in pre-computer tasks can come from a written passage, a tape, a video, an oral interaction, etc. Thus information can be transferred from one medium to another. Finally, some Help information can be provided during the computer activity which aids in the reconstruction of the text, such as tape-recorded hints.

Total-deletion programs are usually authoring programs. This means that users can type in a text of their own, following the instructions in the program and its manual. At first, it is best to type in a paragraph of text, save it (put a copy of what you have written on disc), then see if it works. If it does, you can then write something needed for a lesson. Note that it takes much less time to author your second text, than your first!

Total-deletion programs have been very popular because of the variations of use which such a creator of information gaps can provide. We have shown a variety of lessons using them (see Appendix A for a complete list), and would suggest that you try to understand the general principles involved, and adapt and modify them to your needs. To get you started, here is a sample activity.

5 Invitations

AIM

To consolidate the language of invitations

LEVEL

Elementary

TIME

30–60 minutes

PREPARATION

Hardware
Several computers, and a printer (not essential).

Software
A total-deletion type program.

Knowledge
Teacher — how to author a text. Students — how to use the program.

PROCEDURE

Pre-computer work:
1 Teach students the exponents *Would you like to . . ./How about . . ./Yes, I'd love to/I'm afraid I can't.* Practise in pairs and groups.
2 Get the students to build up the following dialogue, using the discourse chain which is given below:

SAMPLE DISCOURSE CHAIN
Use the following information to construct a dialogue:
Scene: The phone rings in John's house. It is Jane, a good friend.

John	Jane
1 Answer the phone	
	2 Greet
3 Reply	
	4 Invite to go to the cinema
5 Refuse. Grandmother is ill	
	6 Suggest another day
7 Agree. Ask when and where	
	8 Give date and time
9 Confirm then say goodbye	
	10 Say goodbye

Computer-work:
3 Using the discourse chain, and their own dialogue as an initial guess, students reconstruct the dialogue.

Post-computer work:
4 Students should act out the finished dialogue, and devise others of their own making.

MODIFICATIONS

Level
The idea of using a discourse chain as a prompt for reconstructing text can be applied to any text, and thus any level, depending on the degree of difficulty of the text.

Hardware
The lesson could be done with just one computer, with half the class playing one character and the other half trying to guess the second character.

Software
A cloze-type program could be used to do a similar activity, though usually students enjoy completely reconstructing a text.

Procedure
This could be done in self-access, rather than in class. What is most instructive in the activity when carried out in class, is that a simple discourse chain, based on language which has been practised by the students, is a sufficient prompt for the students to complete the task.

A picture or a prompt, or a cassette recording, could be used instead of a discourse chain to give the students help in reconstructing the text.

See Appendix A for more examples of activities using total-deletion programs, and Appendix F for information on total-deletion programs.

1.2 'Office' programs

The activities shown in this section are:
- Word-processing
- Database
- Desktop publishing
- Communications
- Spreadsheets

SUMMARY OF ACTIVITIES:

Program type	Example activity	Level	Time	Name
Word processing	6 Description	I	45–60 mins	'Christopher'
	7 Description	A	55 mins	'My weird neighbours'
Database	8 Numbers	B	20 mins	'Telephone numbers'
Desktop publishing	9 Fluency	E	60 mins	'Wanted'
Communications	10 Oral fluency	I+	75 mins	'EEC Summit'
Spreadsheets	11 Oral fluency	I	90 mins	'Journeys'

Word-processing

Word-processing is one of the most common purposes for which computers are used, and it is probably the most useful program to use when starting to work with CALL.

Word-processing programs come in a variety of shapes, sizes, and degrees of sophistication. Learning to use them can take anything from half an hour to master the basics, up to many hours of practice before mastering some of the more sophisticated functions.

The following are some of the most useful functions which can be found in most word-processing programs. They can be used as a checklist if you are learning to word-process.

1 Learn how to start the word-processor and get into the part where you can start typing – or inputting – text.

2 You need to know how to:
– Type upper- and lower-case letters.
– Delete and insert a letter, a word, a line, and a larger chunk of text.
– Save a text which you have typed (i.e., putting a copy of the text on a disc so that it can be used in the future).
– Load a text (i.e., taking a copy of a text which is on a disc and putting this copy into the memory of your computer).
– Print a text.

Opinions differ as to whether it is best to start with a simple word-processor or with a more sophisticated one, but without using the more advanced facilities initially. We feel that there are arguments either way, but ideally, whether the word-processor is simple or sophisticated, it should be one that is easy to use at the start. The checklist above can be used initially, and, as experience and confidence grow, the following additional functions can be learnt:

- Moving words, lines, sentences, paragraphs and blocks of text around.
- Modifying the presentation of the text (margins, formats, left and right justifications, printer controls, etc.).
- Deleting texts.
- Merging texts.

Some word-processors will also have macros, spelling checkers, and other facilities such as accepting data from other applications packages (see below). The important thing is not to feel intimidated because you do not know how to use all of these functions. You probably also don't know in detail every single new development in language teaching, but it doesn't stop you going into the language classroom.

The basic functions of a word-processor can be used even by someone who is new to computers, if only because they are similar to those of a typewriter (and word-processing is actually much easier than typing, because mistakes can be corrected so easily).

Word-processing is an extremely rich resource, for the following reasons:

1 It is a real tool, which can allow people to do much more conveniently tasks which they would want, or have, to do anyway. This would include the preparation of worksheets and reports, which would otherwise have to be laboriously typed.

2 It provides authentic tasks in the language classroom, since word-processing is a real-world activity.

3 It is a way of developing both fluency and accuracy work from the same material. Some of the lessons, for example, encourage oral and written fluency through creatve writing. These texts can be saved, to be returned to at a future date for accuracy work. (It is normally very hard to pick up the threads of a classroom activity at a later date, but this can be done quite easily with a word-processor.)

Word-processing lessons can be constructed with various degrees of concentration on a text to be created, modified, reduced, expanded, or unscrambled. Alternatively, the main emphasis can be on communicative writing — one group of students sending a letter of application to another, and that group writing a reply; students reading stories written by other groups, and so on.

Many communicative lessons involve the following basic stages:

1 Students start and complete writing a text, in groups.

2 The students save this text.

3 Another group of students get access to this text.

4 They load the other students' text.

5 They perform a task on it — read it, look for mistakes, respond to it.

6 Students read their own, modified text.

To do this, you must be sure of what loading and saving are, as explained above.

It is possible that you are using computers which are separated from one another, or computers which are linked together. If you have a separate computer, a text will be saved on that computer's disc drives. If your machines are connected together, it may be saved on a shared resource. If so, it is easy to load another group's work without physically moving. If you are using separate machines and wish to load another group's work, the groups must either change machines or exchange discs. At first, it is best to do what you find easiest, but we feel it is important to point out that students find it highly satisfying to receive mail electronically, rather than physically.

Here is a basic activity which manipulates a text.

6 Christopher

AIM

To practise the language of personal descriptions and to focus on subject–verb agreement

LEVEL

Elementary

TIME

45–60 minutes

PREPARATION

Hardware
One computer per student or per group.

Software
A word-processing program.

Knowledge
Learners should know how to use the following editing facilities on the word-processor: 'Search and replace'; Delete character; Insert character.

PROCEDURE

Pre-computer work:

1 The pre-computer work for this exercise will depend mainly on the level of the learners and on the content of the text used. The teacher could elicit vocabulary of personal descriptions, and might also want to spend some time on subject–verb agreement (though this is probably best left until after the exercise).

Computer-work:

2 The following text is loaded into the computer(s):

My name's Christopher. I'm 16 years old and I come from Lancaster, England. I live at home with my family — my mother, my father, my brother and sister and my goldfish. I have lots of hobbies. I like football and swimming, and I sometimes go fishing with my friends at the weekend. I'm still at school. I'm in the fifth year at a very big comprehensive school. There are about 2,000 pupils there. I'm not sure what I'm going to do when I leave school.

3 The learners go through the text, changing the details so it describes themselves rather than Christopher. (If this is done individually, the learner will change the text to describe him or herself; if it is done in groups, they can either choose one person from that group, or, if there is time, each of them can produce a copy of the text which describes him or herself.)

4 Once they have changed the details, they then use the 'search and replace' facility on the word-processor to change 'I' to 'he' or 'she' automatically throughout the text.

5 The learners then 'repair' the text by checking punctuation and subject–verb agreement.

6 The learners then save this version of the text, before making the final changes.

7 The final changes to the text involve the learners deleting everything which identifies them directly (i.e., the part which gives their name).

Post-computer work:

8 The task now is for the learners to try to identify whom the texts are describing. Each text is identified (for example, by putting a number on it, or an individual code of some kind), and one copy of the text with the person's name, and one without it, printed out. Copies of the text without the learners' names can be made and distributed to each of the learners (if there are a lot of learners, it is probably quicker to make photocopies); or the copies are passed round from group to group, with each group noting the code for each text, and their guess about whom it describes, before passing it on. Alternatively, copies are pinned on the walls around the room, and learners walk round reading them, noting down their codes and guesses.

9 When they have all made their guesses, copies of the texts with the learners' names can then be collated.

10 The activity can be rounded off with some work on any mistakes noted in the texts. Learners can then be asked to make any corrections necessary, and a final version of each text printed out for each learner to take home.

MODIFICATIONS

Level
This activity can be used at various different levels to focus on various linguistic items.

Hardware
If fewer computers are available, this activity could be done as part of another activity, with learners working on the computer(s) in groups, pairs, or individually.

Software
The lesson does not need any sophisticated word-processing facilities.

Procedure
Step 8 could be carried out at the computer, by getting students to load each other's texts, or exchanging machines.

7 My weird neighbours

AIM

To practise descriptive writing

LEVEL

Advanced

TIME

55 minutes

PREPARATION

Hardware
One computer per group of students; a printer.

Software
A word-processor.

Knowledge
Basic use of the word-processor.

N.B. Before the lesson, the teacher should have written a text on the word-processor. The claim should also have been doing descriptive writing, as part of their course. A suitable frame is:
> *Last week my new neighbours moved in. Being curious by nature, I soon popped round. The most amazing woman answered the door . . . (describe the mother).*
And so on.

PROCEDURE

Pre-computer work:

1 Revise language forms covered during the course for descriptive writing.

2 Explain to the students that they are going to see a text called 'My weird neighbours'. They will be given the story outline, but they should insert the description of the members of the family.

Computer-work:

3 Students in groups write the descriptions. Teacher acts as helper and facilitator.

4 When two groups have finished their description they exchange descriptions and read each other's. If they wish to, they write a critical comment at the bottom of the screen. This could refer to language mistakes, or to the style of the piece.

5 Students return to their original work, and make any changes necessary.

Post-computer work:

6 In different groups, students decide which members of the family were easiest to describe, and why.

7 Students write a similar description for homework.

MODIFICATIONS

Level
The lesson could easily be adapted for lower levels by using more basic vocabulary and patterns in the description.

Hardware
It is important that the writing is done in groups. It is also useful to be able to print out a copy of the students' work.

Software
The word-processor does not need any special facilities.

Procedure
The homework could be written in self-access. The class procedure could be varied a little, by asking each group to slip in one description which actually describes one of the members of the family of one of the students in their group. When the other groups read their text, they have to spot the 'real' description.

See Appendix A for more examples of activities using word-processing programs, and Appendix F for information on word-processing programs.

Database

A database is a program which is used for storing and manipulating information. It stores the information in a similar way to a card-index system of the kind that you might find, for example, in a library. Each card (or 'record') will have details about one of the books, such as author, title, publisher, date of issue, and so on (these are known as 'fields'), and all the cards together constitute the library's catalogue (or 'file'). The way a database stores the information, however, is less interesting than the way it manipulates it. Using a computer, it is possible to search through the records in a file rapidly, and then sort them automatically. A simple example would be sorting the records into alphabetical order, according to the author's name. This can, of course, be done without a computer, but using a database, this sorting can be done both quickly and automatically. More usefully, however, if the records in a file are already in alphabetical order according to the authors' names, and you want them in alphabetical order according to the titles of the books, this can also be carried out quickly and automatically. In other words, the order in which the records are stored in the computer is not important, since they can be re-arranged into any other order almost instantaneously.

In addition to arranging the records in order, a database program allows individual records to be found very quickly. A book by a particular author — someone called Dickens, for example — could be found rapidly; if there are several books by Dickens, the user could specify only books written by Dickens, C., published after 1853 and before 1855, and published in London. Obviously this could be done (and often is done!) without a computer. The significance of a computerized file (or database), is that such searches can be done quickly and automatically, without having to move the records physically as in an ordinary card-index system. Furthermore, the advantages to be gained from using a computerized database, rather than a card-index system, increase, the more records there are.

Databases come in all shapes and sizes, from very simple ones designed for use in primary schools, to powerful ones handling information for large organizations such as banks. The program which is most suitable for a particular file of records will depend on exactly what kind of information needs to go into the records, how it is to be sorted and searched, and how big the database needs to be. A teacher should not, however, feel daunted by this description. We have found that teachers tend to be able to grasp databases more easily once they have become familiar with other kinds of program, but the following is all that needs to be known in order to use databases:

1 How to start a new file.

2 How to design a record by deciding on the number of fields in the record, their length, and their type (for example, whether they are going to contain text or numbers).

3 How to put information into a record.

4 How to save a record.

5 How to alter information already in a record.

6 How to look at records, sort them, and search for information in a file.

On-line information services (see the section on communications), and Viewdata services such as PRESTEL (see the section on VIEWDATA), are all databases and can be very useful sources of information for project work. See Diana Fried-Booth's *Project Work* in this series (OUP 1986).

As well as looking at information already on databases, however, students can also put information into a database, for example about themselves and their fellow students. In addition, they can design their own record, in order to build up a file of information on a topic of their own choosing. Thus the facilities offered by a database can provide the students with tools for tackling problem-solving tasks. Examples of these classroom uses are given in Chapter 2, but the lesson below deals at a fairly elementary level with one of the basic features of a database (and one of the sections in Chapter 3 shows how databases can be systematically used with beginners). Even if you are not teaching elementary students, however, it is worth working through those lessons as a way of learning how to use some of the basic facilities which databases offer.

8 On the line

AIM

To practise asking for names and telephone numbers; the alphabet; numbers 1–10; the uses of *'s* in *What's John's telephone number?*

LEVEL

Beginners

TIME

20 minutes

PREPARATION

Hardware
Preferably one computer per group of three students. A printer.

Software
A database program.

Knowledge
Creating a very simple record with a field for names and a field for telephone numbers.

PROCEDURE

(N.B. The teacher should have prepared the record and file before the lesson.)

Pre-computer work:

1 Revise forms for asking for and giving names, and telephone numbers, plus the alphabet and numbers 1–10. Teach *How do you spell it?* as well.

Computer-work:

2 Students are put into threes at the computer. Student **A** asks student **B** for his or her name; **B** replies; **C**, at the keyboard, listens and types the name in. If **C** can't spell the name, **C** asks **B**, 'How do you spell it?'.

3 Repeat the process, asking, answering, and typing the telephone number.

4 Change the students round, so that **B** asks, **C** replies, and **A** types. Then change so that **C** asks, **A** replies, and **B** types in. In this way all the students have asked for, provided, and typed in some information.

5 The students move from one computer to the next, and repeat the process. Continue in this way until all the names of the class are in each computer.

6 At one computer, sort the records into alphabetical order, then print out the names and telephone numbers and give a copy to the students.

Post-computer work:

7 In pairs, one student has the list of telephone numbers and the other has not: students ask for the telephone numbers of other students; the other students reply. Students can then change roles after a couple of minutes.

MODIFICATIONS

Level
This is a useful lesson to use on the first day of a CALL Teacher Training Course for teachers completely new to CALL. It enables them to break the ice of pressing the keyboard, in the context of doing a straightforward personal-information activity.

If your students find that creating their own information is too difficult at first, you could supply them with information. Put information about different countries into the database (e.g., population, capital, highest mountain, language(s) spoken). The information can then be searched to write comparative sentences or contrasts.

Hardware
One machine can be used. In this case the students can be given the task of going around the class and writing down on paper the names and telephone numbers of their colleagues. While they are doing this, the teacher can put three of the students in front of the computer, and the students do steps 2 and 3 of the lesson. These students can then go back to the classroom activity, and the next group of students come to the computer.

Software
Many computers come with small programs which do the kind of activity presented here without the need for a database: they can be useful in making students become familiar with this type of activity. However, doing this activity on a database is a way of familiarizing students with this type of program, which is an essential preparation for more sophisticated uses of databases.

Procedure
If your classroom is too small to allow all the students to stand up and walk around the room when the lesson is being done with one computer, the activity could concentrate on asking about other students. For example, students can ask and answer, 'What's his/her telephone number?' without moving from their desk, except when going up to the front for their turn on the computer.

Keeping personal information openly available in a self-access facility may not be acceptable in certain teaching situations. If you are considering permanently keeping personal information in a computerized form, you should check whether your country requires you to register the keeping of the information as part of its Data Protection legislation.

See Appendix A for more examples of activities using database programs, and Appendix F for information on database programs.

Desktop publishing / Graphics

Computers are widely used not only for dealing with text and numbers, but for producing graphics as well. One of the principal applications of this graphics facility in the commercial world is Computer Aided Design – or CAD for short. There are many simpler drawing and painting programs available for use on home-computers, though even these are increasing in power to such an extent that the quality of graphics which can be created on some home-computers is very impressive indeed.

One interesting development is the marriage of word-processing and graphics in what have become known as desk-top publishing programs. These provide a range of facilities which enable the user to produce printed material of a quality which previously was only possible through professional printing methods. The combination of text and graphics facilities allows different kinds and sizes of type to be used: text can be printed in columns; shapes and outlines such as boxes and circles can be produced, and can also be shaded; pictures created with drawing programs can be added to the document, and the text arranged around them. Linked to this development has been the falling cost of laser printers, and their increasing sophistication and range of facilities, allowing the full potential of desktop publishing programs to be realized when the document is printed out.

Many writing or project-work activities would benefit from having their final products produced on a desktop publishing package. Chapter 3 outlines such a project, which would be suitable for a group of students studying the media.

It is important to realize, though, that inevitably it takes longer to learn how to use the facilities offered by these increasingly powerful programs. We feel that the use of desktop publishing programs will increase in the classroom when their accessibility, which is determined by their cost, is such that educational institutions use them to produce their own worksheets and pedagogical material. Such programs are excellent for use in production of school magazines. In order to use such a program, however, the teacher or student should have some previous experience of using word-processors and graphics programs.

Here is a lesson to get you started with a simple graphics package.

9 Wanted

AIM

To practise oral and written fluency through designing 'WANTED' posters.

LEVEL

Elementary

TIME

One hour

PREPARATION

Hardware
Preferably one computer per group.

Software
A desktop publishing package.

Knowledge
Teacher or students — ability to use the text and graphics facilities of the package, and link all the different sections together.

PROCEDURE

N.B. Before the lesson, it would be useful for the teacher to have worked out how to do this activity, and to have prepared a sample poster. The poster should not be too good, though!

Pre-computer work:

1 Elicit from students what they know about the Wild West.

2 Show your sample poster. Elicit the purpose of such posters.

3 Ask the students to choose a member of the class and to design a WANTED poster about him or her. The poster should contain a caricature of the person, a statement of their crime, and the reward offered for capture.

Computer-work:

4 Students design the poster, working alternately on the text and graphics parts of it.

5 Print out the posters.

Post-computer work:

6 Pin up the posters round the wall.

7 Students walk round the room deciding if their fellow students are worth the ransom money.

MODIFICATIONS

Level
A more advanced group could design a poster advertising a forthcoming cultural event.

Hardware
It is difficult to do this activity with only one computer, but the size of the groups in desktop publishing lessons can be greater than in most other lessons, as part of the group can be away from the machine in the 'editorial department', discussing the work being produced.

Software

A graphics program could be used to draw the caricatures, which are then put into the desktop publishing package.

Procedure

It is useful to have such packages available in self-access mode, so that students gain familiarity with the program.

The class may well have students who are weak at English, but strong in design skills: lessons such as this create an enjoyable and motivating task for such students.

See Appendix A for more examples of activities using desktop publishing programs, and Appendix F for information on desktop publishing programs.

Communications

In both business and education, microcomputers are increasingly being used as a direct means of communication between users. By linking up machines in different rooms in the same building, or in different buildings, town, and even countries, users can communicate directly with each other by using a suitable program.

1 Communications within the same location

Computers in the same physical building can be connected together with cables to share resources such as printers and hard disc drives, and to send each other messages. This arrangement is called a Network, or, more exactly, a Local Area Network (explained on page 7). Networks have the advantage of enabling all the computers connected to them to have access to all the material stored on hard discs, which have an extremely large capacity.

Manufacturers of networks, or independent software houses, provide software which allows certain types of communication between the machines. A particularly interesting program type is Electronic Mail. This allows system-users to have their own electronic mailbox: letters or messages can be sent to them, or they can send a message to whoever they wish. Additionally, it is possible to have programs which allow instantaneous communication between machines. A user can type, 'What shall we do tonight?' and this will immediately appear on the other machines using the program. We have called this use of the program 'conferencing'. (It should be noted that this term is not being used in the American sense of students and teachers discussing students' written work.)

2 Communications between locations

In addition, it is possible to connect computers using telephone lines. This is done with a device called a modem, which enables a computer to dial up a telephone connected to another computer and transfer information, using the telephone line. A number of electronic services exist (including those designed specifically for educational institutions) to which individuals and institutions can subscribe: using a modem, subscribers can access information held in on-line databases, send mail electronically from one individual to another, and transmit messages for public viewing.

It is important to realize that the programs in this section are of the type which allow information to be transferred. Of course, other program types which transfer or manipulate information can be used to great effect with computers that are linked together. Using a word-processor, texts can be read and altered by other groups at their own machines: viewdata frames (see page 47) can be written at one machine and broadcast to others; databases can be available on-line. (This means that you can access them through a communications link, from your own computer.)

Use of communications programs has not been as widespread as most of the other program types mentioned in this chapter. This is because institutions with Networks tend to be in a minority. However, students find the ability to communicate electronically both stimulating and motivating.

Communications programs have been used not only to link computers in the same building, but to link schools in different countries. This is a particularly interesting development for foreign-language teaching. As might be expected, the practical difficulties are numerous, and such links are better left until experience has been gained with less ambitious projects. If such a link is attempted, it is best to start with something relatively simple and small-scale (e.g., writing a class letter from one class to another) rather than trying immediately to establish links between individual pen-friends.

Using computers in this way provides a means of bridging the gap between the outside world and the classroom, which has been one of the central concerns of language teaching in recent years. The ability of computers to make this contact possible is one of the most exciting aspects of their use in the language classroom.

Here is an example activity for computers linked together in one building.

10   EEC summit

AIM	**To practise the language of formal meetings by simulating a summit conference**
LEVEL	**Intermediate onwards**
TIME	**75 minutes**

PREPARATION

Hardware
One computer per group, linked together into a Network.

Software
An electronic conferencing facility to allow simultaneous transmission of messages.

Knowledge
Teacher and students — using the program to type messages.

PROCEDURE

Pre-computer work:

1 Revise language forms for agreeing, disagreeing, stating an opinion, and interrupting.

2 Announce that there is going to be an EEC summit (adapt as suitable to the country in which you are working).

3 Inform students that fog has meant that the leaders cannot travel to the summit, so it has to take place using computer terminals. Put the students into groups at a machine, and assign a nationality to them. Make one machine the chairperson of the meeting.

4 Give students a few minutes to pool their knowledge of their country. The group who will be the chairperson can work out their rules of conduct for the meeting.

5 Tell students that it is time to submit items for the agenda. Elicit suitable topics for discussion from the students.

6 Allow students a few minutes to decide on their strategy in relation to the topics on the agenda.

Computer-work:

7 The chairperson starts the meeting and introduces the topics. The other groups participate, and the summit is held. The teacher can move round the groups and discreetly encourage the use of the target language.

Post-computer work:

8 The students analyse the aspects which caused most controversy and the effect of the meeting through having it 'on line'.

MODIFICATIONS

Level
The exercise could be carried out by more elementary students using more basic language such as *Yes!*, *No!*, *What!!*, etc.

Hardware
Your hardware may not allow simultaneous broadcasting to all machines, in which case there will have to be short pauses between comments. The facility for different stations to write in different colours is extremely useful. Each group can use a colour from their country's flag.

Software
A facility to record the conversation, so that it could be printed out at the end, would be very useful.

Procedure

This lesson is not suitable for self-access. Writing up the summit as journalists, using a word-processor, in self-access, however, would be a possible follow-up.

The students at the machines should change round from time to time. This could be done in the context of General Election results. It is important that the group acting as chairperson is chosen carefully. Where necessary, help the group to keep the discussion going, and allow only one country at a time to make a comment.

See Appendix A for more examples of activities using communications programs, and Appendix F for information on communications programs.

Spreadsheets

Spreadsheets are another kind of application program, and their main use is to assist organizations and individuals in making decisions which involve extensive calculations. Essentially a spreadsheet consists of a grid which divides the computer screen into boxes (or 'cells'). Information (usually numbers) can be typed into these cells, and calculations performed. For example, seven cells might contain expenditure incurred on each day of a week, and the eighth can contain their total. More precisely, the eighth can contain an instruction which tells the computer that the contents of that cell are equal to the sum of the other seven cells. This is, in fact, one of the most important features of a spreadsheet: the cells are not separate, but linked. The other important feature is that the cells are identified by being given an 'address'. Together these features mean that if, for example, a mistake has been made in the figures for Wednesday, when the correct amount is entered into Wednesday's cell, any other cells in the grid which have information related to Wednesday's cell are automatically changed as well. (There might, for example, be other cells in the grid with a formula for adding up expenditure incurred on all Wednesdays in each month, or on the first Wednesday of each month for the whole year, or for the first half of each week. All of the amounts in these cells could be changed automatically if the amount in one cell for Wednesday was changed.)

This is the essence of a spreadsheet's power. It is possible to experiment with figures to see what effects different ways of allocating resources would have. A practical example would be the ability to calculate wages simply by typing the number of hours worked by staff each week into a spreadsheet containing the formula for calculating the pay per hour for each employee. The amount to be paid could then be calculated automatically. Other formulas would allow the deductions for tax, insurance, and so on to be calculated and deducted automatically.

There has been very little direct use of spreadsheets in language teaching (though it is worth pointing out that a number of simulations are based on spreadsheet programs). This may be due to the fact that spreadsheets normally manipulate numbers rather than words. It may also be because it can be difficult to discover initial uses of a spreadsheet which enable the language teacher to become familiar with its principles.

On the other hand, students may well bring a knowledge of applications programs to the language classroom, and it may be possible to use this knowledge in ways familiar to teachers of ESP (English for Specific Purposes). A spreadsheet might, for example, be set up by the students, who would use English to teach the language teacher a new skill.

Here is an example lesson which uses a Spreadsheet for calculating the financial aspects of a problem.

11 Journeys

AIM

To practise oral fluency through a problem-solving activity

LEVEL

Intermediate

TIME

90 minutes

PREPARATION

Hardware
Preferably one computer per group.

Software
A standard spreadsheet. Current timetables for trains and planes, English Tourist Board Guides to hotels in Britain, entertainment guides, or other suitable authentic material would be useful.

Knowledge
Teacher or students — ability to set up the frame of a spreadsheet. Entering information into the spreadsheet.

PROCEDURE

Before the start of the lesson, the teacher, or students, should have prepared a spreadsheet with space to include transport, accommodation, and entertainment costs.

Pre-computer work:

1 Explain to the class that they have to plan a visit to another country. It could be linked to a school exchange or to a conference, depending on the interests of the students.

2 Ask students in groups to decide on what kind of visit or conference the trip is concerned with.

Computer-work:

3 Put the students at the machines. Hand out copies of timetables and any other material to them. Give the dates of the visit. Explain that they have to plan a reasonable holiday that will not be too expensive, but comfortable and interesting. They have to decide where money and time can best be saved.

4 Students plan their visits, using the spreadsheet to work out the financial details of their visit. One student in each group is given the task of writing down other justifications (as well as financial) for the way the group organizes the trip.

Post-computer work:

5 Students present their trips to each other and discuss which is best.

MODIFICATIONS

Level
This lesson could be done by a more elementary group, practising reading by pointing to the data on the computer, rather than having to explain the data verbally.

Hardware
A printer is needed to print out the spreadsheets. Special printers (136 columns wide) can be bought to print out spreadsheets if you find you are making extensive use of them.

Software
A more sophisticated use of the spreadsheet, once the teacher is familiar with the program, would be possible if the spreadsheet was integrated with a word-processor, so that the financial details could be copied into a word-processor to describe the conference or visit.

Procedure
It would be useful to have the spreadsheet available in self-access, so that students have a chance to familiarize themselves with the program.

A computer could be used in stage 5, during the follow-up discussion, to make minor modifications, if, as often happens, the discussion leads to a compromise involving change to one spreadsheet in order to incorporate the best aspects of several different plans.

See Appendix A for more examples of activities using spreadsheet programs, and Appendix F for information on spreadsheet programs.

1.3 'Library' programs

The activities shown in this section are:

- Viewdata
- Concordancers

SUMMARY OF ACTIVITIES:

Program type	Example activity	Level	Time	Name
Viewdata	12 Persuading	E	55 mins	Sports survey
Concordancers	13 Conditionals	I/A	45 mins	Iffy

Viewdata

Viewdata is a type of word-processing program whose main features are listed below:

1 Information is intended to be read on a screen rather than on paper.

2 The information is intended to be read by large numbers of people, either by placing the screen in a public place, or by transmitting the information to screens in offices or homes.

3 Some types of viewdata are interactive, allowing the viewers to type in responses to the announcements that appear on the screen. (For example, the screen may contain an advertisement for a product: if a keyboard is attached to the screen, the viewer may be able to order the product by keying in a code, such as a credit card number.)

4 Graphic effects can often be mixed with the text on the screen. This usually allows colour, double-height and flashing letters, as well as pictures composed of small blocks.

5 The screens of information (sometimes called 'pages' or 'frames') can either be selected by the user, as each has a unique name or number which can be specified, or they can be set to appear automatically in sequence. (This is usually known as a 'carousel', as the pages appear one after the other until the end of the last one is reached, at which point the sequence starts again from the beginning.) This latter facility can be used to provide electronic noticeboards.

Examples of non-interactive viewdata are CEEFAX and ORACLE (in Britain). Examples of interactive viewdata are PRESTEL in the UK, MINITEL in France, and COMPUSERVE in the United States. These are public services, but in this section we will concentrate on the use of such systems to transmit information within an institution. The section on Communications has already mentioned the use of such programs to communicate with other institutions and countries.

It is important to note that viewdata pages do not actually contain a lot of words (they normally have to be visible to readers standing some distance from the screen): thus, like telexes and telegrams, the medium requires a contraction in the quantity of text, which creates a new style of writing. This in itself can be the basis of part of a writing course. This style of writing is, naturally enough, best practised with our students on the medium in which it occurs.

As these programs are intended for use with the general public, they are designed to be simple to use. Accessing information is therefore not difficult. Nor is it especially difficult for teachers to learn how to author pages of information, though it is useful to have some experience of word-processing first.

If an educational institution is located in a country which has a public viewdata service, then excellent use of such facilities for language work can be made. A simple example would be a lesson in which the weather was a topic: a viewdata page containing the current weather forecast could be used for reading practice—thus achieving authenticity and topicality.

Other uses of viewdata include the creation of 'electronic books', or 'electronic posters', to run information services in institutions. We have done this in our own institutions. Students can assist in writing them: a notice about a film to be shown in the institution, or a party that is to take place, can be written in English by a group of students, to be read by other students — a nice example of a 'communicative' activity. The following lesson provides an example of another use which can be made of this program-type.

12 Sports survey

AIM	To practise writing functional exponents of persuasion
LEVEL	Elementary
TIME	55 minutes
PREPARATION	**Hardware** Preferably one computer per group. **Software** An electronic viewdata system. **Knowledge** Teacher and students — writing screens of text.

PROCEDURE

Pre-computer work:

1 Ask students to write down their two favourite sports.

2 Put the students into groups, according to their favourite sport (or second favourite, if they are the only person to mention a particular sport, or if everyone chooses the same favourite).

3 Explain to the students that they are going to write a page on the computer, advertising their sport and encouraging others to take it up.

4 Students plan the page (including the use of colour and graphics).

Computer-work:

5 Students write their pages. The teacher helps them when they ask for assistance.

6 When the pages have been written, the teacher then links them together.

7 The students then see each other's pages. They have to read them and decide which pages attract them to the other sports.

Post-computer work:

8 Students discuss which are the most attractive pages, and why.

NOTES

The students could be encouraged to write one screen of what becomes an electronic collage of sports, that is, a small part of a much larger whole.

MODIFICATIONS

Level
The task could be varied greatly, according to the level. Somewhat tongue-in-cheek, a course of English for doctors, for example, could write pages comparing various specializations. More advanced students could 'advertise' courses they are studying at university.

Hardware
The lesson could be done with just one computer and a large screen, with one group of students at a time putting their pages in, while the other students work on some other activity.

Software
It would be useful to have a print routine, or a screen dump, to enable the pages to be printed out, so that students can take a copy of their work home.

Procedure
The pages which are written in class could be made available for viewing in self-access mode, or students could work on producing further pages in self-access.

The teacher can write a page, for example, saying that many teachers and students are putting on weight, and need more exercise, and that some students have written suggestions for remedying the situation. Students could then add their suggestions on subsequent pages, working in self-access. We have found it useful to get the students to enter the text of their page on to the screen first, and then add graphics. If classes, especially of younger students, start on the graphics straight away, there is a temptation to get caught up in that and avoid getting round to finishing the text.

See Appendix A for more examples of activities using viewdata programs, and Appendix F for information on viewdata programs.

Concordancers

A concordancer is simply a program which can be used to find all of the occurrences of a particular word or phrase in a text. Essentially it works in exactly the same way as the 'Find' facility on a word-processor: the user types in the word or phrase which he or she wants to find in a particular text, and the program searches through the text, stopping at each occurrence of the word or phrase. The main feature which a concordancer adds to this is the ability to print out the words or phrases it finds, in the context in which they occur. It can print out just the word (or the number of times the word occurs); or it can print out the word with the words which occur just before it and just after it; or it can print out each of the sentences in which the word occurs.

Concordancers have been widely used in linguistic research, mostly for searching through large collections of texts (hundreds of thousands, or millions of words). There are many collections of such texts (known as 'corpora', and usually stored on large mainframe computers in universities), sometimes consisting of a variety of types of text, and sometimes of texts of one particular sort, or on one particular topic.

Largely through the work of Tim Johns at the University of Birmingham, it is now being realized that similar work can be done using the computers which are present in the language classroom. The computer then becomes a resource containing material about the language being studied, to be consulted by teacher and students. One practical use of such a resource would be to relieve the teacher of the time-consuming task of providing authentic examples of certain linguistic features: concordancers allow for concentration to shift from the 'what' of material construction to the 'how' of creating a learning environment.

A concordancing program is a relatively straightforward program. At the time of writing this book, interest in using concordancers in the classroom was considerable, but published versions of concordancers and text corpora for microcomputers had not really started to appear, which had limited the practical experience of their use. Provided that such material does appear in the catalogues of major publishers, we feel that this type of program is one of the most exciting ways of using computers in the language classroom. The following activity makes use of a text concordancer.

13 Iffy

AIM

To provide data for illustrative authentic sentences using conditionals

LEVEL

Intermediate–Advanced

TIME

45 minutes

PREPARATION

Hardware
One computer, with a printer.

Software
A text concordancer.

Knowledge
Students and teachers — interrogating the program.

PROCEDURE

Pre-computer work:
1 Revise the conditional forms covered so far in class. Number them (for example, you may have done first, second, third (and zero) conditionals).

Computer-work:
2 Search for sentences containing the word 'if'.

3 Print out about fifty, or a hundred, depending on the size of the class.

Post-computer work:
4 Cut up the sentences into groups of ten sentences, to give to each pair.

5 Ask the students to look at the sentences and categorize them as 0, 1, 2, 3 or ??? conditionals, by writing the number or ??? next to the sentence.

6 Students do this. When they have finished, they pass their sentences on to the next pair on the right, get another set of sentences, and look at them to see if they agree with the numbering of the previous pair.

7 Repeat stage 6 a few times.

8 As a whole class, on the blackboard, count how many 0, 1, 2, 3 and ??? conditionals there are.

9 If the class are ready for this stage, some of the mixed conditionals could be put on the board, and explained. Otherwise, it is useful to 'admit' to students that the conditional forms they have learnt are not the only conditional sentences used.

MODIFICATIONS

Level
For a simpler search, you could search for sentences containing 'if' and 'would'. Other searches are 'unless' and sentences that begin with 'would' or 'had'.

Hardware

One computer per group would make the search more individual, but it is not essential.

Software

More sophisticated facilities may be available on your concordancer, such as printing out occurrences according to subject areas. This is especially useful for technical searches.

Procedure

Teachers or students can find material, using the program, whether they are doing self-access work or lesson planning.

The extraction of authentic data, once the class is familiar with the program, can be a routine short activity. If you are lucky enough to have a machine in the corner of the classroom permanently available, you can turn to it and run off a few authentic examples of any linguistic structure currently under review.

We feel that it is useful to show students that 'black and white' grammatical rules which they learn in the classroom are simplifications. The purpose is to make the student feel more confident when meeting such forms.

See Appendix A for more examples of activities using concordancing programs, and Appendix F for information on concordancing programs.

1.4 'Home' programs

The activities shown in this section are:

- Adventures
- Simulations

SUMMARY OF ACTIVITIES:

Program type	Example activity	Level	Time	Name
Adventures	14 Oral fluency	I	60+ mins	'Treasure Hunt'
Simulations	15 Oral fluency	I	60+ mins	'If I ruled the world'

Adventures

Adventures have become one of the most popular programs bought for entertainment on personal computers. They typically involve the user in an imaginary world (usually an exotic one of dungeons, dragons, goblins, elves, and various monsters), and solving problems encountered on a journey around that world. The world usually takes the form of a maze, and the purpose of the adventure is to enter the maze – usually in a quest for treasure – to survive the dangers encountered during the quest, and to find a safe way out of the maze. The attraction of the game for the player is the problem-solving or puzzle-solving element, but for the language classroom the interesting feature of these programs is the way the user finds his or her way around the maze. This is done by asking questions, or giving instructions to the computer, either by choosing from a set of options on screen, or, more interestingly, by typing in questions or instructions.

Adventures written for the commercial market tend to be (deliberately) very difficult, and not aimed at those new to computing. There are, however, a number of adventures written for educational use, and these tend to be simpler, though still unsuitable for the initial stages of CALL. In addition, programs are available which make it possible to author adventures: approaching the creation of an adventure as a problem-solving task can be an interesting exercise, both cognitively and linguistically. The use of these adventure–generator programs is still quite difficult, however, and more suitable for more advanced learners.

Despite these reservations, interest in adventures as a form of recreation is widespread. It is therefore worth checking with your students whether they already play adventures, as these are often written in English. We have had the experience of students asking for help with English in order to solve the next stage of an adventure.

Commercial adventures are not often used for language teaching, partly because the language they contain is often seen as too 'exotic' (goblins, elves, etc.), and partly because their complexity makes them difficult for teachers to learn, and time-consuming to use in class. Nevertheless, there are ways round these problems, either by careful choice of the adventure to be played, or by providing help to the learners to reduce the difficulties they will face. Here is an example of a lesson for a simple adventure program which involves finding keys in different locations in order to open a box of treasure.

14 Treasure hunt

AIM	**To practise oral fluency using an adventure**
LEVEL	**Intermediate**
TIME	**1–2 hours (though this depends on the complexity of the adventure)**
PREPARATION	**Hardware**
	Preferably one computer per group of students; tape-recorder.

Software

An adventure, preferably a very simple one. A tape-recording, in three sections, providing clues to help solve the adventure. All three sections together should provide sufficient help to solve the adventure. You also need some dictionaries.

Knowledge

Students — basic principles of adventure programs (moving around the maze, and discovering words the program understands).
Teacher — knowledge of the solution of the adventure, including a map of the world of the adventure.

PROCEDURE

Pre-computer work:

1 Pre-teach any vocabulary in the program which is unknown to students. (With some adventures this will be rather 'exotic'.)

2 Explain the general principle of the adventure. Give students a partial map of the area and a few commands that the computer will understand. Explain the task (e.g., to find the buried treasure).

Computer-work:

3 Students start the adventure and see how far they can get.

4 If students get stuck, allow one member of a group to go to the tape-recorder and hear a conversation between two people which will give them hints about solving the adventure. This student then returns to the group and tells his or her colleagues what information has been discovered.

5 The students continue until they complete the adventure.

Post-computer work:

6 The students check the strategy involved in the adventure, and discuss which elements were most difficult.

MODIFICATIONS

Level

For weaker students, as well as tape-recordings providing clues, dictionaries should be provided for vocabulary help.

Hardware

It is possible to use one computer in solving an adventure, albeit more slowly, with a class divided into teams who take it in turns to move as far as they can until the computer tells them it does not understand their request.

Software

It is worth checking whether any educational adventures have been written for the computer you are using. These may have been written with other school subjects, or students' ages, in mind.

Procedure

Difficult adventures can be left in self-access, so that interested students can spend time learning about the programs.

With adventures that are quite complicated, it will be necessary to spread work on an adventure over several lessons. After each lesson the class could write a short summary of the progress made so far.

Acknowledgement
This example is based on an activity shown by David Eastment and developed by Janet Raynor.

See Appendix A for more examples of activities using adventure programs, and Appendix F for information on adventure programs.

Simulations

Simulations are often similar to adventure programs, and it is not always clear whether a program should be described as an adventure or a simulation. A simulation is a way of reproducing in the classroom as many features as possible of a situation that might be found outside the classroom. Situations that might be simulated include producing radio and television programmes, managing shops or factories, or running a school. However, there are some differences between the two program-types. They are as follows:

1 Simulations are often more open-ended than adventures, dealing with problems to which there is no single correct answer. Whereas adventures are usually based on mazes, and the aim is to find your way safely around the maze and out of it, simulations often present situations in which the user has to decide on a course of action. The computer will then suggest the likely result, and on the basis of that outcome the user will choose a further course of action. An example would be a simulation of running a factory: the user decides how much raw material to buy; how much he or she can afford to pay for it; and how much to sell the finished product for. The program then calculates how many televisions would be likely to be sold at that price (given particular market conditions), and what profit or loss would be made. The user can then decide how to proceed (whether to expand the factory or to lay off workers, and so on).

2 Simulations often deal with problems involving numbers, as in the example of the television factory.

3 Simulations often deal with less exotic topics than adventures, though they are not necessarily more realistic. (While running a factory may be a less exotic situation than one involving dungeons and dragons, it is not necessarily one in which most language learners would find themselves.)

Many simulations are relatively complex, and therefore time-consuming to learn how to use, and to exploit in class. In this respect they are similar to adventures. However, they are usually seen as more 'realistic' than adventures, and we have found them to be popular with many students. They can often be integrated into project work.

Extreme claims are often made for oral work that is or is not done when using simulations. Putting students in groups without any preparation, and asking them to improve their village's, company's, country's well-being, will not necessarily produce discussion. Furthermore, there is a good chance that discussion will take place in the students' mother tongue, in the case of monolingual classes.

In order to produce oral interaction, students will almost certainly need pre-computer activities to warm them up. Similarly, most monolingual classes do not speak in the target language without being trained to do so. Both these factors are true of oral activities in general, and are not peculiar to oral interaction at a computer.

The following activity illustrates a way of using a simulation with a whole class when only one computer is available.

15 If I ruled the world

AIM

To give the students oral fluency practice by getting them to rule an imaginary kingdom

LEVEL

Intermediate onwards

TIME

1–2 hours, depending on whether all the options are carried out

PREPARATION

Hardware
One computer.

Software
A simulation where the students rule an imaginary kingdom.

Knowledge
Teachers and students — entering information into the simulation.

PROCEDURE

Pre-computer work:

1 Demonstrate the program, for one season of the year, putting in some data that will illustrate what happens.

2 Divide the students into groups. Explain that they will have the chance to rule the kingdom, as there is going to be an election to choose the rulers for the next year.

3 Students in groups devise election platforms, making speeches and posters.

4 The election is held, and one group is elected.

5 A village council meeting is held, and policy for the season is discussed. Observers can have the role of reporters. Defeated parties in the election are opposition parties.

Computer-work:

6 One student from each group goes to the computer and watches what happens when the decisions are entered into the computer. They are shown the results page for a minute and have to make notes about what happened.

Post-computer work:

7 The students return to their groups and transfer the information they have obtained to the rest of the group.

8 Repeat stages 5 to 7, using different students in the groups to do the talking or information gathering. As the seasons progress more experience will be available for the students to discuss. Have as many seasons as will give the students useful speaking practice.

9 For homework, the students can write a newspaper report of the island's history during these seasons.

NOTES

This lesson uses the computer for just a few minutes, as part of a much wider series of activities. The computer is in fact used to process the decisions of the students and to act as arbiter.

MODIFICATIONS

Level
The program could be quickly explained in the mother tongue, and then used as number practice for students at elementary and beginner levels.

Hardware
The activity could also be carried out with one computer per group. If so, the teacher may have to move students away from the machines in order to encourage them to discuss their strategy carefully, before they return to type in decisions.

Software
There are many simulations on the market which are of this kind – managing kingdoms, economies, or factories – but the basic principle of deciding where to allocate resources is the same.

Procedure
Complicated simulations could be left for self-access use, to enable some students to familiarize themselves with the more sophisticated aspects of such programs.

There are many possible variations on this particular lesson. For example, each student can be assigned a specific role, such as that of a soldier, so that they are likely to ask for more soldiers as a way of dealing with problems: another can be a farmer, etc. With other simulations, students can take positions in a company, or adopt the roles of ministers in a government, or whatever. The important principle is to create a situation in which there is conflict of opinions, and which will stimulate the search for different solutions to a problem. The computer can then calculate what will be the likely result of the solutions which have been suggested.

Acknowledgement
This lesson was shown to us by Louise Finlayson.

See Appendix A for more examples of activities using simulation programs, and Appendix F for information on simulation programs.

2 Activities

Introduction

Choosing activities

We have organized this chapter so that it should be easy for you to find activities which are suitable for your students. It is divided into the following sections:

1 Grammar exercises
2 Skills practice
3 Lexical activities
4 Learner training

Using the activities

We have described a variety of ways of conducting lessons, with students working as a whole class, in groups, and individually. Sometimes you may have little choice in the techniques you adopt (if, for example, you have only one computer for a class), but most of the lessons can be adapted for situations where only one computer is available, by:

1 Adopting group-work techniques, with one group working at the computer while the others work on other activities.

2 Letting the students all work on the computer task, but in groups away from the computer, with one group at a time sending one or two representatives to key in their responses at the computer.

3 Working as a whole class, with the teacher or one student keying in responses suggested by students.

Program types

The program type used in a particular activity may not be available for your computer, or you simply may not have a copy of all of them. Many of the activities we describe can be adapted for use with other programs, and word-processing software is especially suitable for this. Although the interactive feedback will not be available with word-processing programs, the work that is done on the computer can still be valuable and motivating, but you will have to adapt your techniques to allow for discussion and feedback in class.

If you are not sure what is meant by a particular program type, you should look at Chapter 1, where we describe each of the program types, and provide an example lesson.

Integrating the lessons

It is useful to try the occasional computer activity to build up your own (and your students') confidence, but one of the questions you will want to consider is how to integrate computers into your course, rather than exploiting them simply as a 'novelty' or 'diversion'. The activities in this chapter can be adapted to your own course and linked to more substantial schemes of work. Chapter 3 describes ways of doing this.

2.1 Grammar focus

The following activities are designed to provide students with grammar practice.

16 Question formation

AIM

To practise question formation

LEVEL

Beginner

TIME

45 minutes

PREPARATION

Hardware
One computer per group of students.

Software
A gap-fill type program, which allows phrases and short sentences (rather than just single words) to be blanked out.

Knowledge
Teacher and students — authoring and using the program.

N.B. This activity would provide revision practice after a block of work on question formations.

PROCEDURE

Pre-computer work:

1 Orally revise the question formations which are to be practised.

Computer-work:

2 Students are given a sheet of paper with answers, for example, *I live in London*. They must reconstruct the questions on the computer. As in the example below, students are shown parts of the question to guide them in the production of the full sentence.

Post-computer work:

3 Students design more answers and questions, the answers being typed into the computer using the authoring program. The next class to do the activity can use this material or the original exercise, then produce their own material — thereby creating a chain of material which is produced by one group for another group to use as practice material.

NOTES

The questions can be made more open-ended with more advanced groups, and students can try to be the first group to finish. It is useful to have a printer, to give students a copy of the questions to take home.

This activity could be carried out in self-access. A total-deletion type of program can also be used for the activity, though it is useful to use a program which allows a few words to be shown, for example, names of people and places.

EXAMPLE

The following answers should be on a worksheet handed to the student:

1 Noam Chomsky
2 N-O-A-M   C-H-O-M-S-K-Y
3 The United States
4 Boston
5 Yes, I do.
6 I'm a linguist.
7 In a University.
8 Yes I do.

And students would see the following on the screen:

ON YOUR WORKSHEET THERE ARE ANSWERS TO SOME QUESTIONS. WHAT ARE THE QUESTIONS?

1   What is __ __ __ __   __ __ __ __?
2   How __ __   __ __ __ spell __ __ __ __   __ __ __ __?
3   Where __ __ __   __ __ __ from?
4   __ __ __ __ __   __ __   __ __ __ live?
5   __ __   __ __ __ like __ __ __ __ __ __ there?
6   What __ __   __ __ __   __ __?
7   Where __ __   __ __ __ work?
8   __ __   __ __ __ __   __ __ __ __ __ English?

17 Would you like some?

AIM

To provide students with authentic examples of sentences containing 'some' or 'any' with which to deduce grammatical rules

LEVEL

Elementary

TIME

30 minutes

PREPARATION

Hardware
One computer, and a printer.

Software
A text concordancer (see page 50).

Knowledge
Teacher and students — interrogating a corpus of text.

PROCEDURE

Pre-computer work:

1 Get students to write three sentences with 'some' and three sentences with 'any'.

2 Check them, as a class. Ask students for a rule of use. (You may get 'some' for affirmative sentences, and 'any' for questions and negatives.) Do NOT give any rules yourself at this stage.

Computer-work:

3 Explain to students that they should ask the program to give them ten example sentences with 'some' in, and ten with 'any' in.

4 Students look at the screen, as the sentences are produced. They can also print out the sentences. The teacher should help with any vocabulary. Sentences at a linguistic level much higher than the students can be ignored.

Post-computer work:

5 Students look at sentences and try to deduce a rule of use. They will probably have sentences such as *Would you like some coffee?*, and will eventually deduce that 'some' is the positive word — hence the use of 'some' for politeness in this sentence.

NOTES

There are many different linguistic searches that can be made. Other lessons give more examples, but searches, especially contrastive ones, are limited only by the imagination of the users, and the suitability of the text corpus. However, a concordance program can be more difficult to obtain than other programs mentioned in this book. Check with the major publishers and the main distributors of educational software for your machine to see if one is available.

A corpus of written English, with a Key Word in Context concordance program, is an ideal facility to offer both students and teachers, either in a self-access centre, or in a teachers' room. It can be used to check actual use, and to obtain authentic data for exercises. If students have one computer per group, they can look at the sentences on screen, that is, they do not need a printout. If ten sentences still produce ambiguity, more should be worked on.

18 Test yourselves

AIM

To practise irregular verbs through peer group testing

LEVEL

Elementary

TIME

55 minutes

PREPARATION

Hardware
One computer per group, linked together in a Network.

Software
An electronic conferencing program, which simultaneously enables computers on a Network to send messages to other computers (see page 7).

Knowledge
Teachers and students — using the program.

PROCEDURE

Pre-computer work:

1 Put students into pairs.

2 Give one student in each pair a copy of a list of irregular verbs which have recently been studied.

3 The student with the list of irregular verbs tests his or her partner for five minutes, trying to find as many mistakes as possible. The mistakes should be noted down.

4 Students exchange roles and repeat the activity.

5 After the activity, students tell the teacher the mistakes made and the teacher carries out any remedial work necessary.

Computer-work:

6 Students sit in groups at the machines. At one machine the teacher types *today I go, yesterday I* . . . and asks students to respond. This message will appear on all the other screens.

7 The teacher notes which machine answers first. This machine then supplies another question and notes which group answers first, and invites them to supply a question, and so on. A 'testing chain' is thus created.

8 The teacher can make a note of mistakes. He or she can also join in, if this can be done with the teacher behaving as a student rather than as a teacher.

Post-computer work:

9 For homework, students revise the forms they got wrong, in case the activity is repeated the following week.

NOTES

We deliberately chose a rather mechanical feature – to test irregular verbs – to demonstrate the idea. Stages 3 and 4 can in fact be pair work, preparing questions for students on any language work which the class have studied recently.

In stage 7, it is presumed that the software identifies which machine is transmitting which message. There are three ways of doing this. On some programs, the station number is broadcast: on others, a name chosen by the group is broadcast; finally, if messages can be written in colour, each group can use a different colour.

The particular linguistic feature tested depends on the level. For advanced students, it could be vocabulary, using synonyms as prompts, with care taken to accept all answers which are correct.

When more sophisticated operating systems become available, permitting students to have several programs running at the same time, students could be writing on a word-processor and broadcasting requests for help, or answers to requests for help, to the other groups in the class.

This lesson is not really suitable for self-access, unless there are several machines available in self-access and students wish to test each other in this way. Furthermore, it is useful to have a printer, to print out the interaction.

Stages 6 and 7 can be repeated as a quick revision activity as part of a later CALL class.

19 Reconstruct the story

AIM

To practise narrative writing, and past continuous and simple tenses

LEVEL

Elementary

TIME

60 minutes

PREPARATION

Hardware
One computer per group of students, and one video cassette-recorder.

Software
A total-deletion type program; a video with a short extract on it (1–2 minutes) showing a scene which can be narrated.

Knowledge
Teacher — how to author a text. Students — how to use the program.

PROCEDURE

Pre-computer work:

1 In previous lessons, the past continuous should have been introduced.

2 Show the story on video, without any sound. Give the names of the characters and any unknown vocabulary which students need to know. Get students to reconstruct the story orally, beginning *Last Sunday, . . .*

Computer-work:

3 In groups at the computers, students reconstruct the text which is a narrative summary of the video they have just seen. If students have difficulties, one student from each group can come and look at the video again (the video-recorder should be in another part of the classroom): they can tell the other students in the group what they saw.

Post-computer work:

4 Students could author their own narratives into the program, in a follow-up lesson: they could then act out their story before the other students, and get the others to reconstruct their text orally, then at the computer.

NOTES

This is a lesson which anticipates one of the uses that can be made of interactive video, which is a facility whereby a computer and a video cassette-recorder are linked together: the only element missing in this model is the lack of an interactive link between the video and the computer.

The lesson can be altered by changing the level of language, and it can be done with just one computer and one video-recorder, with students divided into groups looking at the computer and video monitor, then reconstructing the text as a group composition.

20 Presents for all

AIM

To practise asking for information, using the theme of travel

LEVEL

Intermediate

TIME

60–75 minutes

PREPARATION

Hardware
One computer per group.

Software
A specific adventure-type program, called *London Adventure* (see Appendix F, section 13—'Alternatives').

Knowledge
Teacher and students — using the program.

PROCEDURE

Pre-computer work:

1 Hand out maps of the London Underground, and give comprehension questions, for example, *Which line is station X on? How do you get from A to B?*

2 Explain to the students that they are going to travel around London and buy presents for their friends, before leaving the UK.

3 Give students worksheet 1 (appended below) and ask them in groups to spend a few minutes planning their strategy.

Computer-work:

4 Discuss as a whole class a suitable strategy for completing the task.

5 Give students worksheet 2 and ask them to carry out the first task, getting used to the key used by the program.

6 Tell students to 'buy' a tube map and a tourist guide and to use the information in them to plan their route. In addition, tell students that they must write this route down on worksheet 2 and show it to the teacher before starting out on the journey.

7 Students then do the journey. The teacher helps when asked to do so.

Post-computer work:

8 When finished, give students worksheet 3, and check that they have learnt the language needed to carry out the various tasks.

NOTES

It is worth being patient during the start of the computer activity. Students usually take a few minutes to become familiar with the program and are rather silent during this stage. However, once beyond this stage, they tend to get very involved in the program. In fact, one of our Intermediate classes, who had used a fair number of the programs detailed in this book, voted this lesson the one that they had most enjoyed. For a more advanced group, less directed help can be given to students and they can be given the exercise as a problem to solve by themselves.

London Adventure has been produced for several different computers: if you find that it is not available for your machine, it is worth checking to see if a similar piece of software is available for your own make of computer. There is a vast array of commercial adventures for most common computers.

Students could be given the program to experiment with in self-access. This lesson is quite directed: in our experience we have found that this is the most practical way of managing to complete the task within a lesson. If students take longer than expected to complete the journey, stage 8 can be carried out in the next lesson.

Acknowledgement
The worksheets for this lesson were produced by Robert Gizzi and David Forbes.

WORKSHEET 1

Imagine that you are in a capital city that you do not know. You want to do some shopping and some sight-seeing before going home. You have got some traveller's cheques but no cash. You speak the local language. You have not got all day, because you have to catch your plane in the afternoon.

  1 What is the first thing you would do?
  2 How could you get information about something? How many different ways can you think of?

3 When you asked for information, how would you speak?
4 How could you travel round the city? How many different ways can you think of?
5 Which of these would be the quickest/most economical?
6 How could you get information about the transport system?

WORKSHEET 2   London Adventure: Route Planner

1 Get used to the keys.

2 Get some money.

3 Buy a guidebook and map.

4 Use the guidebook and map to plan your journey by completing the chart below.

5 Proceed on the journey, using the second chart to record it. Good luck!

What you need to buy	Where found	Cost	Tick when bought	Nearest tube station
Map				
Guidebook				

Planned Route

From (Tube station)	To (Tube station)	Name of Shop	Buy
1 2 3 4 5 6			

WORKSHEET 3   London Adventure: Follow-up

What do you say in the following situations?

1 You stop a stranger in the street and ask him or her if there's a bank in the area.

2 You ask a stranger for directions to the British Museum.

3 You want to change some traveller's cheques in a bank.

4 You want to buy a guidebook, but you don't know where to obtain one from. Ask a passer-by.

5 You are in a tube station and want to go to Oxford Street.

6 You want to buy a ticket for Oxford Street.

7 You choose a book in a shop and want to pay for it.

21 I am the greatest

AIM To practise superlatives

LEVEL Intermediate

TIME 45–60 minutes

PREPARATION

Hardware
Several computers; one Overhead Projector (desirable), set apart from the computers; printer (optional).

Software
Total-deletion type program.

Knowledge
Teacher — authoring the program. Students — using the program (authoring in the modification).

PROCEDURE

Pre-computer work:

1 In pairs, the students should be given information on the six highest mountains, largest lakes, largest countries, and hottest places in the world. The information can be found in reference books, and presented on graph paper which students could refer to at the computer.

2 One student makes sentences from the data, using superlatives, for example, *Everest is the highest mountain in the world*. The sentence can be either factually accurate or inaccurate: the student can choose. The partner listens to the sentence and says either 'Yes, true' or 'Liar!', depending on whether he or she thinks the statement is true or not. If the partner guesses correctly, he or she can then create a sentence for their partner. The activity continues in this way for a few minutes.

3 The teacher then explains that the students have to reconstruct sentences on the computer which are true facts about the information given to them. Check the ordinal numbers (*first, second*, etc).

Computer-work:

4 Students go and sit at the computers in groups. They then reconstruct the facts about the real world which are in the computer text.

Post-computer work:

5 If students have access to a library, they can then be asked to find out more facts about a different subject, for example, the animal world, and write superlative sentences for homework, or in the next class. Alternatively, the lesson can serve as an introduction to Project Work. See Diana Fried-Booth's book on *Project Work* in this series (OUP 1986).

NOTES

This activity would lend itself to a more advanced class that needed revision of superlatives, in that the 'drilling' is disguised as a 'spot the lying' activity. A fill-in-the-blanks program can also be used, but the students would not get the same satisfaction as they do when reconstructing a complete text. Alternatively, a word-processor could contain a text with true and false facts about the world: this would serve as further practice on superlatives, with students having to delete the false sentences.

A single computer could be used, with groups competing to reconstruct sentences, though this would be less satisfactory than having one computer for each group.

The new information which students write in stage 6 could be authored by them into the program, and then other groups could guess their information, either in class or in self-access, if the school has self-access computers.

22 Maybe

AIM

To investigate the use of modal verbs in the English language

LEVEL

Intermediate

TIME

45–60 minutes

PREPARATION

Hardware
One computer with a large screen, and preferably a printer.

Software
A text concordancer with a corpus of text.

Knowledge
Teacher and students — interrogating a corpus of text.

PROCEDURE

Pre-computer work:
1 Ask students for the 'maybe' auxiliary verbs (*may*/*might*/*could*).
2 Ask students to write a couple of sentences for each, to illustrate the difference in meaning. Discuss possible solutions. Do not give any rules at this stage, though.

Computer-work:
3 Use the program to print out a list of sentences with each of the 'maybes'. Print out about twenty-five occurrences of each verb.

Post-computer work:
4 In groups, give the students five sentences for each example. Ask them to make notes on anything of interest in the sentences, particularly when comparing the other 'maybe' words.

5 Students then exchange their sentences and get more from another group. This process should be repeated several times.

6 Students can then discuss their findings and, with the assistance of the teacher, try to deduce rules of use.

NOTES

The activity could be done at a higher level to investigate modal uses such as *had to* versus *must have* and *needn't have* versus *didn't need to*.

Having more than one computer would be useful in stages 4 and 5, if students wanted access to more sentences to confirm hypotheses. Lists produced by concordancers can be transferred to word-processed files which are then edited.

This kind of exercise is very useful with trainee language teachers, to help them tackle grammar books. If they have formed initial hypotheses of use, the explanations in grammar books will be more approachable. The concordancer may come with other facilities, for example, it may be able to show frequency counts. The program could then be used to find out the frequency of use of *may* and *might*, or *may have* and *might have*. It should also demonstrate other points such as the fact that *can* + participle is not used, but *can* + negative + past participle is.

The software should be available in self-access, to allow students to carry out further exploration of language points which have been studied in class, or which are causing them problems individually. In class, one computer per group would allow students to choose the particular material they wished to search. More ambitiously, with a computer system which allows several programs to work at the same time, a concordancer could be utilized directly from a word-processor, so that students writing texts could check grammatical usage that they were unsure of.

It is worth noting that studies of data obtained in this way have formed the basis of books on, for example, the English modal system. See Jennifer Coates, *The Semantics of the Modal Auxilaries* (Croom Helm, 1983). Clearly, students should not be expected to study at that depth, and strategies for restricting the amount of data presented to students may have to be considered. The beauty of the approach, however, is that students can explore as deeply as they wish to.

23 Finding passives

AIM — To enable the students to consolidate the forms of the passive

LEVEL — Intermediate

TIME — 55 minutes

PREPARATION —
Hardware
One computer, preferably with a printer.

Software
A text concordancer with a corpus of text.

Knowledge
Students and teachers — interrogating a corpus of text.

PROCEDURE —
Pre-computer work:
1 Ask students, in pairs, to write down five passive sentences.
2 Compare them, and divide them into groups according to tense.
3 Explain to students that the class is going to try and find as many passive sentences as possible in the corpus. Elicit what searches it would be most profitable to make.

Computer-work:
4 The searches suggested by the students are carried out, and the sentences printed out.

Post-computer work:
5 Divide the sentences up into groups of ten and give them to the students. Students have to mark the sentences which they consider to be passive, and note down the tense of each, and any other features, including what the text is referring to.
6 Students then exchange their texts, and check each other's opinions.
7 Students' findings should be discussed by the class. It is interesting, for example, to consider which kinds of text contain more passives. In addition, a check should be made to see if any passive forms have been missed, such as the infinitive *to be done*.

NOTES —
Working out how to make a search which will reveal all forms of the passive is itself a good way of revising. With groups studying English for a Specific Purpose, texts from different subject areas could be compared for relative frequency of occurrence of passive sentences. It is worth checking the concordancer to see if it can do multiple searches: for example, *am/is/are/was/were/been/be* and suffix *-ed* will pick up all passives of regular verbs. Finally, having one computer per group would allow the search to be carried out as a group problem-solving task.

24 English connections

AIM
To practise the use of linking words

LEVEL
Intermediate

TIME
60 minutes

PREPARATION
Hardware
One computer per group.

Software
A multiple-choice program, preferably one in which the options appear in context in the sentence (see page 20).

Knowledge
Teacher — authoring the program. Students — using (and optionally, authoring) the program.

Before the lesson, the teacher should have authored material with suitable linking words which have been taught in the syllabus. Sentences should be used which relate to themes which have been covered, or language recently studied, in order to recycle this material.

PROCEDURE
Pre-computer work:
1 Get students to write down all the linking words they know.
2 Group the words into different categories of addition, contrast, result, etc. depending on the particular group(s) which have been studied.

Computer-work:
3 Students do the computer activity, choosing the correct linking word. The teacher helps when asked to.

Post-computer work:
4 Discuss which words caused problems.
5 (optional) Get students to author their own text, using the linking words.

NOTES
The level could be made very simple, using *and, but, also* or very advanced using *notwithstanding, on the other hand*, etc. The activity could be done with a word-processor, but the teacher, or other students, rather than the program, would have to indicate right and wrong attempts.

If you have to do this in class with one computer, and with a young elementary class, you can divide the class into small groups and give each a card with a different connector on it, such as 'and', 'but', 'or', etc. When the sentence requires their answer, one of the group has to rush up to the computer with the card in their hand. This would be a total physical response type activity, and would enable the teacher and students to see if the student was correct. Finally, this lesson can be done in self-access.

2.2 Skills focus

The following activities are designed to help students practise the skills of listening, reading, speaking and writing.

25 Recreate

AIM

To practise listening for numbers in a dictation

LEVEL

Beginner

TIME

20 minutes

PREPARATION

Hardware
One computer, with a reasonably large screen. A blackboard.

Software
A basic word-processor.

Knowledge
Students and teacher — basic word-processing skills.

PROCEDURE

Pre-computer work:

1 Practise the pronunciation of numbers by, for example, giving students cards with varying numbers of items on them and asking them to say what these numbers are.

Computer-work:

2 Divide the class into two teams. Put one student on the computer keyboard, in such a position that she or he cannot see the blackboard. Make sure the other students can see the screen and the blackboard.

3 The teacher writes up various numbers, in numerals on the board.

4 A member of the opposing team to the student at the computer keyboard comes out and writes the number in words. She or he then pronounces it. If correct, the team scores one point.

5 The student at the keyboard hears the number and taps it into the keyboard. If correct, that team scores one point.

6 The class watches for mistakes. If there has been a mistake, the first person to spot the mistake gets a point for their team, and replaces the person at the keyboard.

Post-computer work:

7 The teacher highlights common mistakes which occurred during the exercise.

NOTES

The information-transfer activity can be varied, for example, a phrasal verb can be written on the board and an example sentence has to be written to show the meaning. The student at the computer then has to write another contextual sentence. The principle of the activity, an information-gap between computer screen and blackboard, could be used for other software as well, for example, the blackboard could contain clues for passages with blanks in, using a gap-fill type program.

With two computers, one person from each team could be at each computer, and the activity could therefore become one of speed as well as correctness. Once the activity is in full swing, other numbers can be added to the board by the students themselves.

26 Cross class interviews

AIM

To enable students to communicate from one class to another, using personal information

LEVEL

Mixed

TIME

First activity — 55 minutes for the elementary class
— 10 minutes for the advanced class
Second activity (in another class) — 30 minutes

PREPARATION

Hardware
Preferably one machine per group of students.

Software
A standard word-processor.

Knowledge
Teacher and students — basic word-processing, including creating, altering and saving texts.

PROCEDURE

Pre-computer work:

1 In the more elementary class, revise basic question forms, such as 'What's your name', 'How old are you?', etc. The more advanced class has a lesson on a topic related to their syllabus, as they will only be involved in the elementary students' class for about ten minutes.

2 Get students to devise a grid for asking other students personal information.

3 One student asks another the relevant questions. The other student answers and also listens for any mistakes made by his or her partner. When the first student has asked all the questions, the other points to any mistakes which he or she has made. Students then exchange roles.

4 The elementary class then visits the classroom of the advanced class. The two teachers put students into pairs. The elementary class then interviews the more advanced class.

Computer-work: (Elementary students)

5 The elementary class then goes to the computer room and writes a profile of students they have interviewed. The writing will be done in groups.

6 When students have finished writing their profiles, they then read each others', and take notes on features which strike them about the class as a whole.

7 The class then discuss which of these features should be incorporated into a general description of the other class. They then write the description.

Computer-work: (Advanced students)

8 In another lesson, the more advanced group read the descriptions of themselves. They then extend the description, using more language to amplify these profiles.

9 The groups then read the class profile and discuss whether they agree or disagree with it. They then change it if they wish to.

(Optional further stage for the more elementary class):

10 Students read and comment on the alterations which the other class has made. The teacher helps with language, where necessary.

NOTES

The idea of doing information-gathering activities between classes at different levels, is, we believe, a very powerful one. Typically, the lower class can ask questions, and the higher class answer (as the receptive ability of weaker students is normally higher than their productive ability). Students enjoy the sense of communicating beyond the walls of their own classroom.

The principle of gathering information from a group at a different level can be extended to any level by changing the tasks from those which require the simple asking of yes/no questions, to those which require students to talk closely to other students in order to ascertain their opinions.

Information which can be put into a database (see page 35), can be put into just one computer. (See the Database scheme of work in Chapter 3 for a developed outline of such a use.) This can also be done with a viewdata system (see page 47). Many of the activities mentioned elsewhere in this book result in information which can be made available in self-access. Needless to say, this information can also be read by students at different levels from the original producers.

With large classes at stage 4 it is more realistic for half of the students in each class to change rooms, rather than cram all the students into one room. If there is an odd number of students in a class some repetition in the asking or answering will be necessary.

27 Deep thought

AIM

To simulate a conversation with a non-native speaker of English

LEVEL

Intermediate

TIME

30 minutes

PREPARATION

Hardware
One computer per group.

Software
A simulation program of the Eliza kind (i.e. where the computer engages in a dialogue as an apparent participant). In this specific case the computer is assumed to be playing the role of a job interviewer. See Appendix A.

Knowledge
Teacher and students — typing in responses.

PROCEDURE

Pre-computer work:

1 Ask students in pairs to tell each other where and what they would study, if they were suddenly given a scholarship.

2 Students tell the rest of the class what their partners would wish to do.

3 Explain to the students that they are going to simulate an interview between a student who has just been granted a scholarship, and the computer, which is acting out the role of job interviewer. However, the computer comes from a non-English speaking country and so does not speak English perfectly, and may at times give strange replies. Students should try to keep the conversation running smoothly, so as not to antagonize the interviewer.

Computer-work:

4 Students have their conversations with the computer, in small groups, noting anything unusual in the conversations.

Post-computer work:

5 Put students into different small groups, where they should tell each other about the dialogues they had with the computer.

6 Ask students to decide how the program works and how 'intelligent' they think the program is.

NOTES

In the classic version of Eliza the computer plays the role of a psychiatrist. Several versions have appeared for microcomputers with varying degrees of sophistication. The important point to this lesson is to allow for the imperfections of certain responses on the part of the computer by making it a non-native speaker of English.

More elementary students can have the vocabulary the program uses explained to them before starting the computer activity. In addition, the activity can be done with just one computer and a large screen. In groups, the class can try to predict the next response of the computer.

28 Ideal partners

AIM

To practise oral and written fluency

LEVEL

Intermediate

TIME

60 minutes

PREPARATION

Hardware
Preferably one computer per group of students.

Software
A desktop publishing package; some background music.

Knowledge
Teacher — linking text and graphics; organizing layout.
Students — typing in text and being able to draw.

PROCEDURE

Pre-computer work:

1 Arrange students in pairs (wherever possible, with partners who are good friends).

2 Ask students to close their eyes and be prepared to have a day-dream.

3 Ask them to visualize an ideal friend for themselves and let them dwell on the image of that person for a few minutes. Some relaxing music in the background usually sets the right mood.

Computer-work:

4 Get each student to describe the image of the person to their partner, in as much physical detail as possible. Their partner then sketches this image on the computer, based on the description given by the other student.

5 Students then write a description of the qualities of this special person.

6 Students change places and repeat stages 4 and 5.

Post-computer activity:

7 Pin print-outs of students' work on the classroom walls. Ask them to analyse the similarities and differences between the people described by the students, and discuss these.

NOTES

This lesson can be done in larger groups particularly if there are only a few students who can draw in the class. To speed up the drawing process, it is useful to leave the drawing/desktop publishing package in a self-access area, so that students can become familiar with how it functions.

It may be useful to do one of the icebreaker activities from the *Drama* book in this series (Wessels, 1987) to get the class into a receptive mood for such an activity. If a more conservative idealization would be more suitable for a particular class, an ideal teacher, President, or 'safe' figure could be chosen.

29 Fast food

AIM	**To develop oral fluency by giving the students a problem-solving activity**
LEVEL	**Intermediate**
TIME	**60 minutes**
PREPARATION	**Hardware** One computer per group, preferably on a Network. **Software** A spreadsheet simulation (see page 44). **Knowledge** Teachers and students — entering information. N.B. This lesson assumes that a particular spreadsheet simulation is being used which involves running a fast food stall.
PROCEDURE	**Pre-computer work:** 1 Ask students to write down the number of different kinds of fast food which are (i) locally; (ii) nationally; and (iii) internationally available. 2 Check this list. Elicit the specific characteristics of each kind of fast food. Discuss whether fast food is healthy. 3 Explain to the students that they are going to run a fast food stall at an exhibition, and that they will be doing this in competition with groups at other machines. **Computer-work:** 4 Students start the simulation. It is usually best to let them get used to manipulating the program by going through the first day themselves, then starting the simulation again for 'real', in competition with each other. 5 Students do the simulation, trying at the same time to cheat and see each other's prices. **Post-computer work:** 6 The class compares results, and discusses which strategy techniques were the most profitable.

NOTES

The program can be used with more elementary classes by carefully explaining the task, then getting the students to decide on the numbers and prices for each category of fast food sold. More complicated simulations can also be made available to students in self-access. This would allow a class to use them more quickly, and efficiently. The students who had already used the program could explain it to the other students.

It is possible to do this lesson with just one computer. With a simulation lasting six days, the class can be divided into six groups and they can each have a day in which they try to make as much percentage profit as they can.

30 Yes minister

AIM

To practise oral fluency through giving students the task of managing a national economy

LEVEL

Advanced

TIME

75 minutes

PREPARATION

Hardware
One computer with a large screen.

Software
A spreadsheet simulation which manages a national economy.

Knowledge
Teachers and students — entering information into the program. Some basic understanding of Economics.

PROCEDURE

Pre-computer work:

1 Ask students, in pairs, to draw up a list of what their, and most governments, spend money on. Provide them with vocabulary such as *defence, social services, law and order*, etc.

2 Feed back this information to the whole class. Discuss to what extent spending is due to political pressures and/or other reasons.

3 Explain to the students that they are going to manage a national economy.

Computer-work:

4 Take students through a sample year, showing them all the decisions which have to be made.

5 Give students in small groups a few minutes to decide on the policy their group wishes to follow. Give them the chance to work out arguments in favour of their policy, and help with suitable language.

6 Ask students to imagine that the current government of their country is a coalition. Before the meeting, they should practise expressing their ideas, and ask the teacher to clarify any language problems.

7 Have the formal budget meeting.

8 Students vote on the best policy, then enter it into the computer.

Post-computer work:

9 Students see the effect of their decisions, then analyse the results, and repeat steps 5 to 8.

10 Students set the scenario to continue for a few years, then have a concluding discussion to decide what they have learnt about managing the economy.

NOTES

Whilst there may not be a simulation specifically connected with managing an economy for the machine you are using, most machines have several simulations which require budgeting decisions to be made. If it proves impossible to find one, a spreadsheet could be used for projections of expenditure.

This is another example of a simulation which is processing the students' decisions, but where the decision-making can take as short or as long a time as students wish, as it can be done away from the machine. Students should be encouraged to role-play the cabinet meetings in as realistic a way as is consistent with their language abilities.

Simulations such as these are often quite complex. Making them available for students to use in self-access can cut down on the time needed to familiarize students with the program.

31 Reading about London

AIM

To give the students intensive reading practice

LEVEL

Elementary

TIME

90 minutes

PREPARATION

Hardware
One computer per group; tape-recorder.

Software
London Adventure (see Appendix F, Section 13—'Adventures');
listening tape; dictionaries.

Knowledge
Students and teachers — using the program.

PROCEDURE

Pre-computer work:

1 Play listening material which practises finding and giving directions on the London Underground.

2 Revise ways of expressing requests.

Computer-work:

3 Students in groups read the program instructions on screen and work out how to use the program. They then check their understanding of it with another group. Dictionaries can be used if needed.

4 Students work through the program, making sure that they understand what is happening at each stage.

Post-computer work:

5 Students should be given the chance to ask for help with any linguistic misunderstandings they may have.

NOTES

We have deliberately included two different activities for a piece of software such as 'London Adventure' (see page 64) for the other activity). Software can be expensive, and it is possible to use it with different levels, in different ways.

The ability to read, understand and react to information in English on a screen is increasingly important in a variety of fields.

Acknowledgement
The idea of using this program as such was thought up by Louis Gillespie.

32 Censuses

AIM

To practise reading for information and written narrative, using census information

LEVEL

Intermediate

TIME

55 minutes

PREPARATION

Hardware
Preferably one computer per group.

Software
A simple database with a file of information about people who lived in the past, for example, census returns for a village; word-processor.

Knowledge

Teacher and students — searching for information on a database; basic word-processing skills.

PROCEDURE

Pre-computer work:

1 Get the class to write down what they consider to be the three most important differences between their own life and the life of someone their age a hundred years ago.

2 Compare and discuss the opinions.

Computer-work:

3 Students should be given the names of a family from the past. They search the database to find out as much information as they can about the family and their circumstances.

Post-computer work:

4 Students write a narrative on the word-processor describing the family, and the lives they led, using the information obtained from the database.

NOTES

With a more elementary class, a narrative writing task could be done by giving students a parallel text about another family as an example. This activity can also be useful in helping students develop an understanding of a society. For example, census information about a village in Dorset around the time of Thomas Hardy's *Tess of the D'Urbervilles* might help students reading that novel to develop an understanding of the society in which it was set. The activity can also be suitable for students studying the theme of the Industrial Revolution. (Studies could be made of the occupations of villagers, as opposed to town dwellers, whether the children at certain ages were at school or working, etc.)

It is worth contacting the major publishers to see if they have any census data (real or imaginary) available for the students to use. If not, the teacher could consider creating an imaginary community from the past or, better still, get one class to research the period, and create an imaginary population which can then be used by another class. The information should also be available on a self-access basis, so that extra tasks could be set for students who either wanted or needed them. If you have a library, the tasks could also be linked to available reference material on the period.

The activity could be done with one computer and a large screen. Groups of students could be given different characters to look for. Information about various characters could be presented on the screen for a short time, and the activity could thus become a scanning task.

Banks of information for this kind of application are likely to become more widely available as a result of developments in CD ROM and Interactive CD and Video.

Students could put in information about themselves in order to compare and contrast their own lives. Note though, that some countries, such as the United Kingdom, have Data Protection Acts, which oblige any institution recording personal information to register this activity with a Governmental Agency. If in doubt, check the position in your country with an education adviser.

33 Note-taking

AIM

To practise making notes from a text

LEVEL

Advanced

TIME

30 minutes

PREPARATION

Hardware
One computer per student, pair or group; printer.

Software
A word-processing program.

Knowledge
Using the delete and insert editing facilities on the word-processor.

N.B. The text to be studied should be available on paper and on screen.

PROCEDURE

Pre-computer work:

1 The teacher discusses the topic of the passage, to prepare students for the subject matter.

2 Students read the passage in print, and prepare to ask the teacher questions to elicit information which will give the teacher some idea of the students' understanding of the text.

3 Students skim-read the passage, and give a summary of its contents.

Computer-work:

4 The students work in pairs, groups or individually with a copy of the text on their computer. First of all they read through the text quickly and select the main points.

5 Then they go over the text again, deleting the parts which are not relevant.

6 They re-read the text to check that their notes are adequate. At this stage it is useful to print out a copy for them to read and check.

7 Then they go through their notes again, tidying them up so that they are clear and easy to follow.

Post-computer work:

8 The notes produced by each group or individual student are printed out, and copies distributed to each of them.

9 The class then reads through each version of the notes and writes down anything they think is wrong or that could be improved upon. (They are here concerned with accuracy of content, rather than spelling, punctuation, vocabulary or grammar.)

10 Students then do a final revision of their notes, save them, and print out a copy for themselves.

NOTES

Different word-processing programs allow different ways of editing text. Some allow text to be highlighted or marked in some way, for example, by altering the colour of the text, underlining it on screen, or changing the background colour of parts of it. If these facilities are available, it is better to use them until students are satisfied they have the final version of their notes: when they are satisfied with their choices, they can then delete the parts they don't want. Working in this way means they can reverse changes they have made more easily should they decide to.

The activity involves stages, such as editing, which can be done on paper or on screen. We suggest you experiment to find the most satisfactory combination.

34 Famous people

AIM

To practise summary writing in order to produce a radio and newspaper biography

LEVEL

Intermediate

TIME

90 minutes

PREPARATION

Hardware
Preferably one computer per group; tape-recorder with recording facilities.

Software
A standard word-processor; biography of a famous person.

Knowledge
Teacher and students — basic word-processing skills; how to record audio material onto a cassette.

PROCEDURE

Pre-computer work:

1 Tell the students you are going to write a name on the board, and you want them to write down the first thing that comes into their mind. Put up the name of the famous person and give the students a maximum of ten seconds to write a response.

2 Put students' responses on the board, then discuss them.

3 Divide up the biography and give each pair of students a few pages.

4 Students read their part of the text carefully and write a short summary of the essential biographical information. The teacher helps with language when asked to do so. Check that students don't just copy from the text, but use their own sentence patterns.

Computer-work:

5 Students then type their summaries into the word-processor. It may be necessary, because of the number of machines available, to put two pairs of students together. If so, each pair can check each other's text.

6 While some students type their summaries, the others record their biographical summaries on the tape-recorder. These must be in chronological order, and the first group should write a short introduction to the radio programme.

7 When students have finished typing in their text, they should prepare comprehension questions on their material. Encourage them to prepare one question which can be best answered by reading the text, and one which would be answered by listening to the programme. The one for reading can be added to their word-processed text. The one for listening can be written on the board.

Post-computer work:

(This may carry over to another lesson, if the class are not used to word-processing.)

8 Students use their own radio programme as a listening comprehension exercise, and answer the questions.

9 The teacher prints out the texts and arranges them as a collage on the wall. At the start of the next lesson, students read the text and answer the reading comprehension questions written by the other students.

NOTES

A very different biographical summary can be written for advanced students. For example, advanced literature students can be asked to comment on the biographical situation of authors, at key points in the development of their writing, comparing and contrasting such periods in the author's life. Furthermore, the file-merge facility, which many word-processors have, can be used to combine all the students' texts into one long text file.

Texts with comprehension questions can be made available for self-access reading. These can be set either as homework for the whole class, or as useful supplementary work.

35 Dialogue reordering

AIM	To practise sequencing a dialogue (using a standard textbook dialogue)
LEVEL	Elementary
TIME	50 minutes
PREPARATION	**Hardware** One computer per group. **Software** A word-sequencing program or a word-processor. **Knowledge** Teacher — authoring the program. Students — using the program. N.B. Before the lesson, the teacher should author sentences which form a conversation between characters from the students' textbooks.
PROCEDURE	**Pre-computer work:** 1 Elicit from students what they know about the characters in the dialogue, based on previous units of the book. 2 Explain to the students that they are going to see jumbled-up words which form sentences that they have to put into correct order. **Computer-work:** 3 Students unscramble the words of the sentences, and write them down in their notebooks. **Post-computer work:** 4 Students put the sentences into the order in which they think they were spoken. 5 Get each group of students to act out their version of the dialogue. Meanwhile the other groups listen and note down any differences between this version and their own. When all the groups have given their dialogues, the class decides on the correct order. 6 If there is time, the students can write a continuation of the dialogue.
NOTES	This activity deliberately has two stages of unscrambling — words at the computer, then sentences away from it. More difficult texts can be created using short extracts from real plays. (Some good examples occur in the volume on *Drama* in this series.) The activity could be done with a word-processor which would then enable both the word and sentence unscrambling to take place at the computer. Students should then be encouraged to add the names of the relevant speakers at the start of each sentence.

An interesting variation on the idea can be created with a class using two computers. One of the computers has all of the sentences for one of the speakers in a dialogue, and the other computer has the sentences for the other speaker. Students must sequence the words, then sentences on their own computer, and finally guess what the other speaker says. Students can then be paired off, one from each group, to see how close they got to the actual dialogue.

36　Personal letters

AIM

To practise language to extract personal information, and to use this information to write penfriend letters

LEVEL

Elementary

TIME

55 minutes

PREPARATION

Hardware
Preferably one computer per group.

Software
A database program, with an integrated word-processor.

Knowledge
Teacher — setting up the database and knowing how to put information from the database into a word-processed letter. Students — inputting the information into a database.

PROCEDURE

N.B. The teacher should have set up the database file before the start of the lesson, and the model penfriend letters as well.

Pre-computer work:
1　Revise the question forms for personal information, for example, 'How old are you?', 'Where do you live?', etc.

Computer-work:
2　In groups of three, students type in their information in the following way: Student A asks Student B the questions; Student B responds and Student C, at the keyboard, types in the information. Repeat twice more, with the students assuming different roles. They then go into new groups and repeat the process.
3　The teacher then transfers the information in the database to the word-processed letter and prints out the penfriend letters.

Post-computer work:
4　Students read their letters and if they are acceptable, post them to real penfriends.

NOTES

The ability to transfer information from a database to a standard letter requires a certain degree of familiarization with your software.

With more advanced classes, the basic letter that is produced can then be extended on the word-processor. This lesson benefits from being done with a good applications package.

With just one computer on a Network, small groups can be taken to the computer one at a time whilst the rest of the class are obtaining the information. The letter can also be sent using an electronic mailing facility on a Network, thus enabling students to write such letters in self-access.

If the students do not have real penfriends, they can simulate the process by acquiring penfriends from other classes, and changing their names to fictitious ones. Correspondence can be maintained, and helped, by the teachers. Towards the end of term, students can arrange a social occasion, and actually meet their penfriends.

Acknowledgement:
We would like to thank Joseph Rezeau for showing us how basic information compiled by a class on a database can be used in a penfriend letter, as the following shows.

Example model:
Dear <PENFRIEND>
My name is <NAME>. I was born on <DATE OF BIRTH>, so I am <AGE>. I have got <BROTHER> brother/s and <SISTER> sister/s. My father is <OCCUPATION> and my mother <MOTHER OCCUPATION>. I like <LIKES> and I dislike <DISLIKES>. I live in a house with <ROOMS> rooms. My home is situated in <REGION> and it's in a town of <POPULATION> inhabitants.
I've got <PETS>. My favourite singer is <SINGER>.
I hope you can write soon.
Regards,
<NAME>

37 Letters of application

AIM	To practise letters of application
LEVEL	Intermediate
TIME	75 minutes
PREPARATION	**Hardware** One computer per group preferably, but not essentially, linked together in a Network. **Software** A word-processor. **Knowledge** Basic use of the word-processor.

PROCEDURE

Pre-computer work:

1 Either from a suitable textbook, or using an authentic text, present students with a letter of application. Give the students tasks which allow them to focus on the formal style of the letter.

2 Hand the students recent job advertisements, and ask them to choose the job they would most like to have.

Computer-work:

3 Students write their letters of application on a computer, as a group-writing exercise.

4 When students have finished their letters, they save them. Then they load another group's text . They read the text carefully, and, depending on the quality of English, write a letter asking the person to come to an interview.

Post-computer work:

5 Students conduct job interview role-plays, alternating between applicant and interviewer.

NOTES

In order to make the activity more realistic for teenage students, ask them to imagine that it is ten years into the future. Tell them they have had a marvellous ten years with all their dreams coming true! In pairs, students should tell each other about the marvellous time they have had, and then use their experiences as material in the letter of application and in the interview.

When doing writing tasks which will be seen by other groups, it is better to create a clear system for naming files. The simplest method is naming by numbers. If possible, write a number clearly on your computers: students can use this number for naming their files. Another possibility is using the name of one student for each group, so long as this will not lead to two texts having the same name. The teacher should keep track of the names, so that he or she can tell the groups the name of other texts which they can read.

Groups work at different speeds. However, the first group to finish usually does not have very long to wait until the second group finishes, and then they can exchange texts. Whilst waiting for another group to finish, the first group can look for ways of improving their text.

The task can be made more difficult by concentrating on the realism of the activity, and the type of job students apply for, for example, a translator, a teacher of English, a tourist guide, etc. Furthermore, this lesson does not require any sophisticated word-processing facilities.

This activity is chiefly concerned with skills needed for writing letters of application. A useful lesson to accompany it is one which helps students write curricula vitae on a word-processor.

With one computer, the letters would have to be staggered and written one group at a time, while the other students work on another activity. As this lesson relies a lot on communication between students, it is not suitable for self-access. However, students often ask teachers for help in producing first drafts of letters on word-processors.

38 Self-ish

AIM — To practise describing people

LEVEL — Elementary

TIME — 55 minutes

PREPARATION — **Hardware**
One computer per group of students.

Software
A standard word-processor.

Knowledge
Teacher and students — basic word-processing skills.

N.B. This is a good lesson to use when introducing students to the basic skills of word-processing outlined on page 30.

PROCEDURE — N.B. Before the lesson, the teacher should type in or prepare a text similar to the one reproduced below.

Pre-computer work:

1 Students match the questions to the description on the worksheet appended.

2 Get students in pairs to choose someone in the class and describe them. The teacher goes round the class and helps with any problems.

3 Ask students to describe orally the class members they have chosen. Then give their oral descriptions. The teacher notes down common mistakes.

Computer-work:

4 Take students through the steps which are necessary to load the text which is on the worksheet.

5 Show students the basics of word-processing.

6 Students alter the text so that all the sentences describe one person in their group.

7 Students then save their text. Make sure that each group uses a different name, for example, the name of one student in each group.

8 Students then exchange discs or machines with another group. On a Network, students look at the catalogue of texts and choose one which another group has written. They then load it.

9 Students look at the text, and try to guess who is being described. They write that guess at the end of the text, and save the text under its original name.

10 Students then repeat steps 8 and 9 with another text, adding their guess after another group's guess. They repeat this exercise as many times as their interest, or the lesson time, allows.

11 Students load their original text and see if other groups managed to guess their description.

Post-computer work:

12 Students tell each other who was being described in their descriptions.

13 If there is time, the teacher can highlight some typical mistakes made by the students.

NOTES

The key elements of this lesson are personalization of a text and information transfer. However, the same exercise can be used for more sophisticated descriptions. For example, in a class of advanced students, the descriptions that students have to alter can contain either too many sentences or too many pronouns (i.e. she . . . she . . . she), so that students have to improve the style, as well as alter it to describe one of them. Style checkers or thesauruses can be made available: the latter are particularly useful for advanced descriptive writing.

A self-access bank of descriptions of famous people could be constructed, for example, as a class competition. Students could write the descriptions in class, and they could be stored on self-access machines for reading and guessing by other classes.

If it is the first time that the class has word-processed, do not take more than a few minutes with the pre-computer activities. They may need some time to get used to the basics of word-processing. Activities 8 onwards can always be done in another lesson.

EXAMPLE TEXT

Part 1

Look at the following questions and match them with the sentences in part 2.

1 What are you wearing?
2 What is your hair like?
3 How tall are you?
4 What colour are your eyes?
5 What do you look like?

Part 2

Read the following description and change it to describe one of the students in your group.

1 I'm about 5′ 6″ tall.
2 I've got dark, straight hair.
3 I've got blue eyes.
4 I'm wearing blue jeans and a bright green anorak.
5 I'm rather short and I've got a round face.

39 Tourist guide

AIM

To write a tourist guide to a city

LEVEL

Elementary upwards

TIME

1 or 2 lessons (depending on research time)

PREPARATION

Hardware
One computer per group of students.

Software
A standard word-processor.

Knowledge
Basic word-processing skills.

N.B. The teacher or resources room should ideally have some tourist brochures in English about the students' country or town. Often, a textbook will have a text in the style of a tourist brochure, which can serve as an introduction to the activity.

PROCEDURE

Pre-computer work:

1 Hand out the information from the tourist brochures, along with some skimming questions.

2 Elicit from students what tourists may be able to do in the chosen area, or in different geographical regions in that area. Give each group a particular topic, for example, sports facilities, eating out, museums, music, parks, nightlife, etc.

3 Explain to the students that they are going to write two paragraphs about their particular topic on the word-processor.

Computer-work:

4 Students write up their part on the word-processor. Encourage them to mix, offering advice to each other.

5 When students have finished, they should look at each other's texts, and make either linguistic or factual comments in order to improve the texts.

Post-computer work:

6 Print out the texts and put them onto a collage which the other classes can see.

7 For homework, students can be asked to extend the paragraph they wrote in class, by finding out more information. If students enjoy the activity it can be continued during another lesson, using the information which they had managed to find out between classes.

NOTES

The main idea behind lessons such as this is that each group of students should write a piece of work, which can then become part of the accumulated efforts of all the groups. The material can even be sent off to a publisher of a tourist guide of the country in question. One of the authors did this with a class, and the work of the students was acknowledged in print in the Second Edition of a tourist guide (Mark Ellingham and John Fisher, *The Rough Guide to Portugal*, Routledge and Kegan Paul.)

Very elementary classes can even correct wrong spellings of words in their own language in the guide, or update the prices of food. More advanced classes can discuss topics such as architectural styles. The activity is of course very useful for groups of students who are studying to be tourist guides. If you are linked to other schools through electronic mail (see page 7), especially in other countries, this would be useful material to exchange. In addition, it would be useful to have a desktop publishing program to publish such work.

This is difficult to do with just one computer in the class though it can be done on a self-access basis, with one initial section provided as a model along with suggestions and instructions on how to extend the text. It may be more interesting to get students to write short guides to places they have visited. This can form a much larger part of a project on the country. For ideas see the book on *Project Work* in this series (Fried-Booth, 1986).

40 Passives and processes

AIM

To practise the use of the passive, and sequencing adverbs, in descriptions of processes

LEVEL

Intermediate

TIME

60 minutes

PREPARATION

Hardware
Preferably one computer per group; printer optional.

Software
Total-deletion type program; cut-up pictures showing a process.

Knowledge
Teacher — authoring a text. Students — using the program.

PROCEDURE

Pre-computer work:

The teacher should author into the program the text which students will have to reconstruct.

1 Give each group a set of pictures showing a process. Tell students to arrange the pictures in the order in which the process takes place.

2 Check the order. Elicit from students an oral description of the process using sequencing adverbs (e.g. firstly, secondly, after that, etc). Show the use of the passive in such descriptions.

Computer-work:

3 Get students to reconstruct the text at the computer.

Post-computer work:

4 Give students a print-out of the answer and discuss what caused difficulty in the reconstruction.

5 Students can themselves construct a text for other groups to guess, in a future lesson. Alternatively, they can be given another set of pictures and, either in class or for homework, construct a description.

NOTES

This is an intermediate exercise, if the language focus is on the use of the passive. It can also be a more advanced exercise if the style of process descriptions is being focused upon, or more elementary if the cut-up pictures are based on a narrative which the students have to reconstruct (see Activity 19).

The lesson can be carried out in a modified way with a 'fill in the blanks' program, but not as satisfactorily. Alternatively, a word-processor could be used for putting sentences describing the process into the correct order.

The exercise can be done with one computer and a whole class, with a large monitor or TV screen. For a process involving six stages, give each group one picture and a couple of minutes to prepare a description of their picture. Each group then gives their description, orally, and then students decide on the sequence of the pictures. (If it is difficult this way, each picture could be stuck on the blackboard, or even drawn there to start with.) Each group then goes to the computer and types in their part of the process. Students can then write another description.

A useful technique, if the text is based on a tape-recording, is to put a cassette-recorder in one part of the classroom and let one student from a group use it when that group needs help. Only let one student from each group go the cassette-recorder: he or she has to listen and then report back to the other students on what he or she has heard.

41 Five in one story

AIM

To practise creative narrative writing

LEVEL

Intermediate

TIME

60 minutes

PREPARATION

Hardware
One computer per group, linked together in a Network.

Software
An electronic conferencing program, which enables computers to send messages to other computers.

Knowledge
Teachers and students — using the program.

PROCEDURE

Pre-computer work:

1 Give students five characters/objects which must be included in a story, for example, frog/red car/Maria/Stockholm/a castle.

2 Explain the procedure. The class is going to write a story which will include the five elements. The teacher will start the story with a sentence followed by . . . . (four dots). Any group can then type the next phrase. Once one group has started, the other groups must wait until they see the . . . . prompt before continuing. In this way, only one group is writing at a time.

Computer-work:

3 Start the story off with a sentence, for example, 'The red car had broken down . . . .'. Let students carry on. If the story falters, the teacher should help by supplying the next phrase.

Post-computer work:

4 Students recapitulate the story.

5 Students can write up the next part of the story or a story with another five objects.

NOTES

This can be done with a word-processor and just one computer, with students in groups each suggesting the next sentence, and the class deciding on which suggestion should come next.

Acknowledgement
The idea of using five elements in a story comes from John Morgan and Mario Rinvolucri, *Once Upon a Time* (Cambridge University Press, 1983).

42 The American tourist

AIM   **To practise narrative and descriptive writing**

LEVEL   **Intermediate**

TIME   **1 hour for writing. 2 hours, with editing**

PREPARATION

Hardware
A computer network, with one computer per three students.

Software
Word-processing program with a merge facility.

Knowledge
Teacher — using the word-processing program, including merging different parts of texts into another text. Students — using the word-processor for basic editing.

PROCEDURE

Pre-computer work:

1 Explain to the students that they are going to write a dictation on the computer.

Computer-work:

Dictate the following phrase: 'Once upon a time an American tourist came to . . . (their city).' Tell students to decide if the tourist is a man or a woman and then tell them to describe the view of the city from the air, concentrating on the organization of the physical description.

2 Students discuss the description and then write it.
N.B. This can take about 15 minutes.

3 The teacher then dictates: 'After arriving, the tourist picked up the bags, which were damaged, and then went through customs and out into the late afternoon sun of the city. S/he jumped into the first cab and told the driver to head for the . . . hotel. Only after a few minutes did s/he realize how strange the driver was.'

4 Ask students to describe the cab driver, concentrating particularly on use of vocabulary. Again, this can take about 15 minutes.

5 Then dictate the following passage: 'S/he finally arrived at the hotel and went up to her/his room. The hot shower came as a welcome relief. Rested and refreshed, the tourist started out on one of the most romantic and adventurous nights of her/his life.'

6 Students are then asked to write the ending to the story, concentrating on making the story as interesting as possible. Teacher helps with vocabulary when asked.

7 After students have been writing for nearly an hour, warn them that they must come to the end of their story, and allow them time to do so.

8 Ask students to change the 'Once upon a time' opening into something more original and creative.

9 Students save their texts, using different names for each text. (A unique first name is usually the easiest name to use.)

10 Get each group to load a text written by another group as follows:

Group A — wrote text 1, now edits text 2.
Group B — wrote text 2, now edits text 1.
Group C — wrote text 3, now edits text 4.
Group D — wrote text 4, now edits text 3.
etc . . .

Explain to the students that they are going to edit another group's text, making notes on paper, but *not* altering the content of the text in any way. Each student is given a number (1, 2 or 3) and assigned one of the following tasks:

Student 1 looks at the text for linguistic accuracy.
Student 2 looks at it and assesses the strengths and weaknesses of how the text is organized.
Student 3 makes notes on how interesting the story is, and on the quality of vocabulary used.

11 After students have done this, they tell each of the other members of their group their findings. The other students have a chance to reread the story and carry out the other two tasks to see if they agree with the findings for each category. The editing notes are then written at the end of the story, and saved.

12 Students are assigned a different editing role to the one they had before. They load their own texts. Then they discuss whether or not they agree with the editing notes. The group then has an editorial meeting with their editors.

13 Students then edit their stories.

14 Students take on the third editing role and read the other groups' stories.

Post-computer work:

15 For homework students can add more steps to the story and more physical and character descriptions.

16 The teacher can take all the groups' descriptions of the city from the air, or from the cab driver's point of view, and copy them into another text file, so that they are next to each other. They can then be looked at as a whole for positive and negative aspects.

NOTES

With an advanced class, all the activities can in fact take several lessons. Indeed, it may be better in some cases to do the story in stages, writing only a physical description, then a description of place, then narration, then concentrating on the beginnings and endings of stories. In this way, the writing syllabus work linked to a book such as *Writing in English 3* by Anita Pincas and Gillian and Charles Hadfield (Macmillan, 1982) can build up to quite an extended piece of work.

The Network allows students to look at other students' work with ease, and allows the teacher to merge parts of texts written at several different machines. Coupled with assigning different roles to students, and writing and reading editors' notes, communicative information gaps and transfers are generated, and reasons for discussion caused by differences of opinion are created.

43 Did the butler do it?

AIM

To practise oral fluency in problem-solving, then to practise reported speech in writing up a police report

LEVEL

Intermediate

TIME

55 minutes

PREPARATION

Hardware
Preferably one computer per group.

Software
A crime simulation.

Knowledge
Teacher and students — knowing how to use the program.

N.B. This activity assumes a simulation where suspects, located in various locations, provide different alibis to a police inspector. The inspector then uses the inconsistencies of the suspects' statements to discover who committed the crime.

PROCEDURE

Pre-computer work:

1 Ask students to tell you about Agatha Christie and her writings. Mention other crime writers, who may be well known to the class.

2 Explain to the students that they are going to wander round a mansion trying to find a thief. When they meet thieves, they should write down their location and their alibi.

Computer-work:

3 The students go round the locations in the simulation, noting down the occupants' alibis as they wander round the mansion.

4 They try to discover the person who has committed the crime.

Post-computer work:

5 Students write up an account of their discovery of the thief, in the form of a police report. Remind students that the alibis should be written using reported speech.

NOTES

The lesson has a distinct fluency stage — discussing where to go, and whether occupants are innocent or not; and a distinct accuracy stage — writing up the police report, and using reported speech.

It is worth checking the major educational software publishers (see Appendix D) to see if they have a program like this for your machine. Some simulations of this kind can be authored, and students find it amusing to have the suspects become fellow students in their class. It can also be enjoyable for a group of teachers learning to use computers, to solve a crime in which their colleagues are the suspects.

It can be useful with more complicated simulations, to allow some of the students the chance to familiarize themselves with the programs in self-access. These students can then help the others in becoming familiar with the programs. The lesson can also be done with just one computer, in which case, after each new alibi is read, the class should be encouraged to speculate on the identity of the thief.

If one group finishes before the others, they can be sent to other groups to play the role of 'teacher' — guiding the class to the solution. Care should be taken to verify whether the simulation is random or not, that is, a different thief every time. If the group that has not finished has a different thief, this could cause confusion (though this can and has been exploited as an information gap).

2.3 Word focus

The following activities help students with both the single and the textual use of words.

44 Sound me out

AIM

To give pronunciation practice

LEVEL

Any

TIME

20 minutes

PREPARATION

Hardware
One computer per group.

Software
A gap-fill type program, which can be authored.

Knowledge
Teacher — authoring the program. Students — using the program, for the main activity; authoring for the variation.

PROCEDURE

Pre-computer work:

1 Explain to the students that they are going to see a number of groups of words on the screen. All except one word will have the same middle vowel sound. They have to discover which word this is.

Computer work:

2 Students complete the exercise and write down any words which they were not sure how to pronounce.

Post-computer work:

3 The teacher checks the words students have written down and uses this as a basis for further pronunciation work.

NOTES

The main aim of this activity is to give students an alternative way of focusing on pronunciation of phonemes. The activity must be followed up with oral pronunciation work. When linked to other activities, the computer *can* in fact be used to help speech and pronunciation. The particular pronunciation feature can be varied, depending on the needs of students. For example, sentences can be given, and the blanks could contain the stressed words of those sentences.

If you have no authoring program, the activity could be replicated on a word-processor, without the interaction of an authoring program. It is useful if the gap-filling program has an option to hide the length of the word.

This activity can be done in self-access, but it needs to be followed up in class. One computer with a large monitor can be used with the class split up into two competing groups.

Acknowledgements
The idea of using a gap-filling program to practise pronunciation was shown to us by Peter McCreadie.

Example:
INSTRUCTIONS
This program will help with pronunciation.

Read the words in each list and decide which *one* is pronounced in a different way from the others. The different one is the one you type.
FOR EXAMPLE:
raid   ride   paid   way

YOU TYPE:
ride
Say each word before you type. GOOD LUCK

start   heart   short   part   /✱✱✱✱✱✱✱✱/
write   right   height   eight   /✱✱✱✱✱✱✱✱/
speak   break   take   shake   /✱✱✱✱✱✱✱✱/
go   show   do   sew   blow   /✱✱✱✱✱✱✱✱/

taste   cast   waist   waste   /★★★★★★★★/
owe   you   low   throw   /★★★★★★★★/
through   threw   bought   clue   /★★★★★★★★/
palm   calm   warm   harm   /★★★★★★★★/
caught   through   bought   thought   /★★★★★★★★/
wrong   young   tongue   sung   /★★★★★★★★/
earth   birth   north   worth   /★★★★★★★★/
gone   won   son   nun   /★★★★★★★★/
lie   buy   high   way   shy   dry   /★★★★★★★★/
rare   bear   hair   share   near   /★★★★★★★★/
sheep   ship   cheap   sheen   /★★★★★★★★/
though   rough   enough   stuff   /★★★★★★★★/
spear   wear   dare   prayer   /★★★★★★★★/
drum   come   thumb   home   /★★★★★★★★/

45 Spell it write

AIM

To practise spelling

LEVEL

Any

TIME

20 minutes

PREPARATION

Hardware
One computer per group.

Software
A gap-fill type program, which can disguise the length of the answer.

Knowledge
Teacher — authoring the program. Students — using the program.

N.B. Before the lesson, the teacher should have authored material containing typical spelling mistakes from the class.

PROCEDURE

Pre-computer work:

1 If the words on the computer are linked to a certain type of spelling problem, for example, doubling consonants, features and rules, they can be revised before the computer activity.

Computer-work:

2 Students are given a list of words on screen. Some are spelled correctly and some are spelled wrongly. If students think the word is spelled correctly they just type a full stop (.) If the word is spelled wrongly they type out the correct spelling.

Post-computer work:

3 Students make notes of the words they spelled wrongly and show them to the teacher.

NOTES

When authoring, it is important to remember just to put a full stop in the gap when the word is correct, for example, careful / . /, and the correct spelling if the word is wrong, for example, writting / writing /.

This activity can be done at any level, with tasks ranging from spelling numbers, doubling consonants, and irregular plurals, to spelling words which cause particular difficulty to your students. A word-processor could be used instead, but without the interactive element.

Many classes contain one or two students whose spelling is considerably worse than the other students. The busy teacher often recognizes this, but does not have time to do very much about it. A bank of spelling material on computer would be useful for such students, for both class and self-access activities. In class, the activity could be done by just one student or group of students, while the other students are doing a different activity. Here is an instance of one possible use for a single computer in a classroom.

Acknowledgement
The idea for this lesson was shown to us by Vanessa Burke.

46 Numbering

AIM

To practise forming numbers

LEVEL

Beginner

TIME

30 minutes

PREPARATION

Hardware
One computer per group of students.

Software
A matching program which allows multiple matching (see page 23).

Knowledge
Teacher — how to author material using the program.
Students — how to use the program.

N.B. Before the lesson, the teacher should have authored the material to be used.

PROCEDURE

Pre-computer work:

1 Revise the pronunciation of numbers with students.

2 Put column A and column B on the board, as shown below. Explain to the students that they must choose one item from each column to make a number. If they choose numbers less than ten, they finish the number with a full stop (.)

Computer-work:

3 Students try to find as many numbers as they can, noting which attempts are correct and which are wrong.

Post-computer work:

4 Tell students to write down the numbers which they couldn't make from the lists, for example, forty.

The lesson should highlight the spelling of eleven, twelve, thirteen, fifteen, twenty, thirty, forty, and fifty.

NOTES

The activity could be done with one computer and a large screen. Divide the class in half, and make one half responsible for the 'teens' and one for the 'tys'. The class has to go through each number and say if it can be made from the information in the columns.

A word-processor could be used to give the stems, then students could write out the possible words. However, since it is such a common exercise-type, students are likely to find the interaction and immediate feedback of a matching program more motivating.

This material could be available for self-access work. Finally, more work could be done on the oral pronunciation of numbers, or, as a supplementary activity using a word-processor, students could take it in turns to give number dictations to other groups.

The material to be used for the lesson is:

A:	**B:**
one	.
two	teen
three	ty
four	
five	
six	
seven	
eight	
nine	

47 Negative prefixes

AIM

To practise the use of the negative prefixes un-, in- and im-

LEVEL

Intermediate

TIME

55 minutes

PREPARATION

Hardware
One computer per group.

Software
A matching program which allows multiple matching (see page 23).

Knowledge
Teacher — authoring the program. Students — using the program.

PROCEDURE

Pre-computer work:

1 Put the prefixes on the board.

2 Elicit examples of words which begin with each prefix.

3 Explain to the students that they are going to see a list of these prefixes on the computer, and a list of stems. They should match a prefix and a stem where appropriate. Point out that there may be more than one possible use of a stem.

Computer-work:

4 Students do the activity.

Post-computer work:

5 Discuss which answers the students found difficult.

NOTES

The exercise can of course be done with suffixes as well. A word-processor could be used by requiring the students to make a list of all the possible answers, then getting the teacher or other students to decide if the students' list is correct. This would not be as satisfying as a dedicated program, though. Lists of words beginning with un- in- or im- could be produced from the spelling checker of a word-processor.

The exercise could be done with one computer and a large screen. This material would be suitable for self-access use. In addition, students can also author the material, for other students to guess.

48 Translations

AIM

To use a total-deletion type program as an aid to learning translation techniques

LEVEL

Advanced

TIME

60 minutes

PREPARATION

Hardware
One computer per group.

Software
Total-deletion type program.

Knowledge
Teacher — authoring the program. Students — using the program.

PROCEDURE

N.B. The teacher should have authored suitable material before the lesson.

Pre-computer work:

1 Revise the translation technique which is being concentrated on.

2 Give students a handout with material to be translated on it. Explain to the students that they will have to reconstruct the translation on the computer.

Computer-work:

3 The students reconstruct the translated text.

Post-computer work:

4 Students discuss which particular features of the passage were difficult to translate, and acceptable alternatives to the computer version of the translation.

NOTES

The translation could be done at any level. For example, it could be 'Hello, What's your name?' for beginners, up to a modern rendering of a classical play (i.e. the activity could even involve 'translating' from archaic to modern English).

There are different opinions in language teaching concerning the value of translation, and the same considerations apply to computer activities. For further ideas, see Alan Duff's *Translation* in this series (OUP 1989).

A word-processor could be used for a similar activity, though without an interactive element. The difficulty of the task of translation with an advanced class creates enough discussion for the activity to be a productive one, even with just one computer.

49 Sexist

AIM

To practise reading for specific information, and to discuss how social attitudes influence language

LEVEL

Intermediate onwards

TIME

55 minutes

PREPARATION

Hardware
First part — one computer and a large screen.
Second part — one computer per group; a printer.

Software
A standard word-processor.

Knowledge
Teacher and students — basic word-processing skills for creating, altering and saving text.

N.B. Before the lesson, the teacher should have typed in an advertisement for a job which asks for either a man *or* a woman to fill the post, and another advertisement which specifically asks for one or the other sex.

PROCEDURE

Pre-computer work:

1 Give a list of job titles for men. Ask for the female equivalents of, for example, policeman, air steward, tailor, etc.

2 Point out that: (i) English does not always show gender morphemically, for example, a student can be a male or a female; (ii) the male gender tends to be used for generalizations: 'man proposes, God disposes' . . . ; (iii) in recent years there has been a move amongst certain sectors to use words such as person; and (iv) the sex discrimination act in the United Kingdom makes it illegal to advertise for one sex only.

Computer-work:

3 Show students the advertisement on the screen, and get them to alter it so that it does not seem specifically to ask for either women or men. One student at a time can make an alteration. The rest of the class can observe and comment on the alteration.

4 After this students form groups and analyse a text which uses lots of male forms to make a generalized statement.

5 Students then alter the text so that it is neutral using forms such as 's/he', or pluralizing to 'they'.

Post-computer work:

6 For classes who are interested in the cultural aspects of language, students can discuss to what extent this general use of male forms influences social behaviour.

NOTES

Elementary students need only be required to change *he* and *she* forms to *they*. Advanced students can look through texts for more suitable forms of discrimination. A very advanced group may like to discuss ways of avoiding clumsy 'non-sexism', for example, through the use of the passive voice. The search facilities of a word-processor can be used in an interesting way in such a lesson, for example, to load up several texts and search for *he*, then *she*. Count up the number of occurrences of each, and see if any conclusions can be formed. (Look at the content of the texts as well to see if this accounts for any discrepancies.) Concordancers can also be used to search for these features.

A printer would be useful to print out the finished comments. It would be possible, though obviously not as ideal, to do the second computer activity with just one computer and a large screen. Instead of removing and changing the forms *he* and *she*, the sex of a character in a narrative can be changed: alternatively, the nationality of a character can also be changed.

50 A computer in the hand

AIM

To practise English proverbs, and give an advanced class oral fluency practice in an intellectual discussion

LEVEL

Advanced

TIME

90 minutes

PREPARATION

Hardware
One computer per group of students; printer desirable.

Software
A sequencing-type program.

Knowledge
Teacher — authoring the program. Students — using the program.

PROCEDURE

Pre-computer work:

1 Students write down as many English proverbs as they can, individually.

2 The teacher checks these.

3 The teacher explains how the program works (i.e. which keys put the jumbled words into the correct order).

Computer-work:

4 Students unscramble the sentences, and write them down in their notebooks. The teacher helps with any problems.

Post-computer work:

5 Students try to understand the proverbs, with the help of the teacher.

6 Students discuss if similar proverbs exist in their own languages. (For example, the English 'to kill two birds with one stone' in Portuguese is 'to kill two rabbits with one stick'.) If there is a similar proverb, students should transliterate it into English.

7 The whole class compare their findings. The teacher can then explain any indecipherable proverbs.

8 The class can then discuss the reasons for cultural differences between proverbs. Many proverbs will be seen to have religious backgrounds, agricultural origins, etc. (See Kavin Blast, *Tasks and Meanings*.)

NOTES

The activity can be done with one computer. In that case, as much discussion as possible during the computer stage should be encouraged. In addition, the activity could be replicated on a word-processor, though without the interaction of a dedicated program.

2.4 Learner training focus

The following activities are designed to help students monitor their progress.

51 Look what I've learnt

AIM	**To help learners become more aware of their linguistic progress**
LEVEL	**Any**
TIME	**Occasional periods of ten minutes**
PREPARATION	**Hardware** One computer, preferably with a printer. **Software** A basic database. **Knowledge** Teacher — creating the record structure. Students — inputting and searching for information.
PROCEDURE	N.B. This is not a lesson as such. It is useful to start doing this a few hours after the beginning of a course.

Pre-computer work:

1 Make sure students are aware of the linguistic aims of the course. If using a textbook, show them the structural, functional index, vocabulary items, etc., or else show them your own syllabus plans for the course. Explain to them that the idea of using the database is to help students and teachers to chart their progress throughout a course.

2 Get students to write down as the course progresses their own self-assessment of how well they know particular items from the syllabus, on a scale of one to ten. Students should also write down a number indicating priority for further study. (See example database.) A low number would indicate a high priority.

Computer-work:

3 Students key their assessments into the database. This should include brief comments.

4 If students are motivated to do so, they can also use a word-processor to keep a diary of their learning.

Post-computer work:

5 The database can be used by students and teachers as a basis for feedback on both learning and teaching, and the devising of relevant activities for the rest of the course.

For complete beginners, the descriptions of the fields could be in their mother tongue (if the computer supports that language's script). A far more sophisticated logging of learning, including student self-assessment and teacher assessment is possible with database management systems which have the capacity for a large number of fields per record, and are therefore able to contain data on a large number of linguistic items. It would be useful to have an integrated software package, so that the information from the database could be transferred into the word-processing diary of the student. As an alternative to databases, this procedure could also be used with a spreadsheet.

This can be done as a self-access activity. We would suggest, though, that it is initially done in class to help students familiarize themselves with the activity.

Another possibility is to compute the averages of one item to discover areas for revision. In addition, extra fields could store test results. Comparisons could then be made to discover where there were areas of disagreement between students' self-assessment and test results.

Example database:

STUDENT NAME: JOAN SMITH

CLASS: PX28

LANGUAGE ITEMS:	KNOWLEDGE	STUDY PRIORITY
1. EXPRESSING OPINION	– 5 –	3
2. PHRASAL VERBS	– 2 –	1!
3. VOCAB – TALK –	– 8 –	8
4. REPORTED SPEECH	– 5 –	5
5. REQUESTING	– 9 –	9
6. EXAM TECHNIQUE	– 1 –	1!

STUDENT COMMENTS: In week three I did a lot of work on ways of REQUESTING. This area is now O.K.

TEACHER COMMENTS: Would you like some extra work on PHRASAL VERBS? Try the exercises on self-access material, course PX28, item 43.

52 Shields

AIM

To practise oral and written fluency in the context of a 'getting to know you' activity

LEVEL

Intermediate

TIME

60 minutes

PREPARATION

Hardware
Preferably one computer per group of students.

Software
A desktop publishing package.

Knowledge
Teacher — linking text and graphics; organizing layout.
Students — typing in text and drawing a graphic image.

PROCEDURE

Pre-computer work:
1 Explain to students that they will be drafting work on paper which will be transferred to computer.
2 Students draw a shield on a piece of paper (about as large as a page in this book), and divide it into four equal sections.
3 In the first quarter, students write down the names of three people who have had a strong influence on them.
4 In the second, students draw and label three things that they are good at doing.
5 In the third, students write down the name of a place where they have been happy, and a place where they have been sad.
6 In the fourth, they write down a hope and a fear with regard to the future.
7 Finally they write a motto under the shield.

Computer-work:
8 In groups, students type and draw each others' shields into the computer, whilst explaining their contents to each other.

Post-computer work:
9 The shields can be printed out, and copied, so that an introductory booklet about the class can be produced.

NOTES

The teacher can draw blank shields before the lesson, for classes that would not have time to draw them within a lesson. They could then be filled in by students. It is preferable to let students draw their own shield, however.

Other personal information can be used in place of the suggested items.

Acknowledgement
The shield's activity was shown to us on paper by Cynthia Beresford of Pilgrim's School, Canterbury, Kent.

53 Personal news

AIM
To allow students to have a forum to communicate in English, amongst themselves.

LEVEL
Any

TIME
Open

PREPARATION
Hardware
One computer.

Software
An electronic viewdata system (see page 47).

Knowledge
Teacher — setting up the facility for the students.
Students — authoring and linking pages.

PROCEDURE
N.B. This is an activity which is not done in class.

Pre-computer work:

1 The facility for a student electronic noticeboard should be created.

2 Find some students who would be willing to learn how to write, edit and link pages, who could get the system off the ground, and provide help notes for other students.

Computer-work:

3 Students write pages. For instance, each week could be the subject of a particular theme, for example, life at home, difficulties in learning English, advertisements for selling textbooks at the start of term, and so on.

Post-computer work:

4 Try to get the other teachers in your educational establishment to encourage students to write and read information on the system.

NOTES
This facility allows students to have their own English language forum. It also allows students to teach their colleagues a skill. There may come a time when the notion of censureship will have to be considered.

There is always the danger that the system may be used to produce text which is offensive to certain students (and parents and teachers!). Again, it should be made clear to students that it is a public system. Therefore, individuals who think that something is offensive should feel that they have the right to delete that particular piece of information, whether they are students or teachers.

Elementary students should be encouraged to write simple information on the system — likes and dislikes is one possibility. If the viewdata software includes a printer routine, pages could be printed out, and displayed on 'normal' noticeboards.

If there are several machines available for self-access in an Institute, one could be a dedicated machine, broadcasting information about the Institute's cultural or extra-curricular activities, and another could broadcast the students' electronic noticeboard. If the machine(s) which contain the students' electronic noticeboard are on a Network, and the Network has a modem which is used for electronic communication with other schools (see page 7), then pages could be transmitted to other educational establishments.

Whilst this is not meant as a class activity, if students wish it, information produced could form input for discussions, scanning practice, and so on. The important principle is not to do anything which criticizes the information, or is seen to 'spy on it'.

54 Book reviews

AIM

To allow students a chance to write book reviews for other students

LEVEL

Elementary onwards

TIME

Open

PREPARATION

Hardware
One computer in a self-access facility.

Software
An electronic viewdata system.

Knowledge
Teacher — setting up the system. Students — authoring and routing pages.

PROCEDURE

N.B. This is an activity which is not done in class.

Pre-computer work:

1 Advertise in the institution that a certain computer is available for students to write book reviews. Alternatively, have a competition, with a prize for each level, to write book reviews within a certain period of time.

2 Students choose a book and read it.

3 They prepare a short review of the book, including a number between one and ten for how interesting the book was (i.e. 10 = very interesting; 0 = incredibly boring), and a letter indicating how difficult the English of the book is (i.e. A = very difficult; E = very easy).

Computer-work:

4 Students write reviews on the computer. An example could be provided for those students who need a model to follow.

5 The reviews are then linked together.

6 Students read other reviews and decide which is going to be their next book.

Post-computer work:

7 When students have finished their next book, they can write their own review of it, if they discover they disagree with the opinion of the original review.

NOTES

The stage of starting to read English books, whether simplified readers, or authentic novels, is an extremely important one. Students very often ask the teacher for recommendations, and the teacher usually has only his or her own 'reading for pleasure' experience to draw on. This activity creates a bank of reviews by fellow students, which can be of real use to them. The possibility of a student reading a book and disagreeing with the original reviewer, and then writing another review of the book means that the process is thus seen to be interactive, where each student's opinion counts.

Book reviews can also be written on a word-processor. With a Viewdata program, it is not difficult to link them together (press '4' for fourth year book reviews, etc.), and so they can be browsed through more easily. On the other hand, book reviews for advanced students may be longer, and suit a word-processor better.

A review can be written by a student at any level. With higher levels, the review can not only be orientated towards literary criticism, but towards helping the teacher with reading suggestions. (We find that student book reviews are a useful help in deciding our own reading.) If the viewdata has a carousel feature – the ability to automatically display a number of pages for fixed periods of time – then recent reviews can be highlighted.

This activity is meant for self-access, but can also be done in a lesson. In fact, it is important to do this occasionally, to stimulate students to read. If the computers are connected up in a Network, it is easier to read material produced in different parts of the building. (For example, book reviews produced in a computer room, or a self-access centre, can be transferred over the Network, from one place to the other.) Reviews should be short, so that they are seen as a communal source of help with reading, rather than as a chore.

Acknowledgements
The idea for grading both enjoyment and linguistic difficulty in this way was suggested to us by Peter Goode. The competition idea was suggested by Paul Seligson.

55 Homework projects

AIM

To allow students to word-process their homework

LEVEL

Any

TIME

Indefinite

PREPARATION

Hardware
One computer system.

Software
A standard word-processor.

Knowledge
Students — starting up the system, and using the word-processor.
Teacher — loading the students' work, and editing it.

PROCEDURE

N.B. This is an activity which is not done in class.

Pre-computer work:

1 The facility should be set up (e.g. class discs can be left in a suitable place, such as a reception area). In places where discs may not be completely secure, students could be asked to leave some form of identification as a deposit for a disc.

Computer-work:

2 Students type in their homework.

Post-computer work:

3 Other students, or the teacher, look at the text and edit it.

NOTES

When institutions consider setting up CALL, one of the first thoughts is of setting up a self-access facility. Typically, many plans have to remain on ice, as there is not enough non-teaching time in the institution to produce sufficient material for these projects. Using this sort of activity, however, it is only necessary to set up the administration of the facility, then the institution has 'productive' self-access, where students are supplying the material.

The level depends on the difficulty of the homework task which has been assigned. More advanced students would benefit from word-processing facilities such as an on-line thesaurus, spelling-checker and style-checker. Teachers worried about the help which these facilities give the students should consider that more and more students will have facilities such as these in their homes. Students can in fact produce 'pre-checked' and 'post-checked' versions of their homework.

In institutions where students do a lot of word-processing, it may be necessary to keep one floppy disc for each student, to prevent other students from accidentally deleting each other's work.

This facility should only be provided if students have the chance to take away a printed copy of the text.

Peer correction, or teacher/student discussion can be done in the classroom, for example, with the rest of the class doing another computer activity. The editing stage is very flexible, and depends on the philosophy and practice of the teacher and students.

It is necessary to be aware, however, of the new range of technological excuses for not doing homework: 'My disc was full . . .', 'The dog chewed up the disc', etc.

56 Student worksheets

AIM

To allow students access to word-processing their own worksheets

LEVEL

Any

TIME

Open

PREPARATION

Hardware
A computer with a printer.

Software
A word-processor.

Knowledge
Loading, editing and saving texts.

PROCEDURE

N.B. This is an activity which is not done in class.

Pre-computer work:
1 The facility for students to write their own material should be set up. This could involve setting up a collection and distribution system for floppy discs, or allocating students space on a Hard Disc on a Network.

Computer-work:
2 Students write in their material. A typical exercise might be students typing in a currently popular song, with blanks to be filled in.

Post-computer work:
3 The worksheet is printed out, photocopied, given to students, and the work done in the class. Alternatively, if the work is CALL material, it is done on computer.

NOTES

The activity can be done in class, but as a student rather than as a teacher-initiated activity. Care should be taken in deciding, for example, which parts of a song to take out. Various effects can be achieved by taking out verbs, adjectives, or one 'actor's part' in a song which tells a story. Similarly, it is sometimes useful to give the whole verse and then delete the whole chorus.

Acknowledgement
The idea for this activity came from one of our classes. They wished to finish the week off with learning the words of a new song. The idea of producing their own worksheets had been initiated by their previous teacher, Charles Cummins. The natural extension was to be able to word-process the worksheets.

57 Find the mistakes

AIM

To help students identify typical mistakes

LEVEL

Any

TIME

45 minutes

PREPARATION

Hardware
One computer per group of students.

Software
A multiple-choice program, preferably where the options appear in context (see page 20).

Knowledge
Teacher — authoring the program. Student — using the program.

N.B. Before the lesson, the teacher should have authored the material which the students will use.

PROCEDURE

Pre-computer work:

1 Tell students they are going to see sentences containing alternatives. One of the alternatives is wrong: they have to find out which one it is.

Computer-work:

2 Students try to find the mistakes. The teacher gives assistance when requested.

Post-computer work:

3 Students write down five mistakes they have made recently which they would like to have included in the next 'find the mistakes' lesson.

4 This information is then shared with the whole class.

NOTES

A normal multiple-choice activity usually gives one correct answer along with several wrong answers. By giving one wrong answer and several correct ones, we are explicitly forcing students to focus on the wrong item. One way students stop making mistakes is by realizing something *is* a mistake.

The level can be adjusted by varying the difficulty of the mistakes.

An interactive program such as this allows attention to be drawn explicitly to an error. It can then lead on to the next activity, which involves error analysis on a word-processor. One of the most useful banks of material to have in a self-access facility is a 'find the mistakes' series of exercises created in this way.

58 Correction strategies

AIM

To develop students' correction strategies

LEVEL

Any

TIME

55 minutes

PREPARATION

Hardware
Preferably one computer per group.

Software
A standard word-processor.

Knowledge
Students and teacher — basic use of a word-processor, including loading, altering and saving of texts.

N.B. Before the lesson, the teacher should have written a text, which incorporates some of the mistakes recently produced by students.

PROCEDURE

Pre-computer work:

1 Tell students they are going to see a text containing mistakes, based on their recent writing mistakes. Ask them in pairs to write down and predict five mistakes which they think the text will contain.

2 Compare student predictions and find out which mistakes are judged to be the most common.

Computer-work:

3 Students work through the text, finding the mistakes.

Post-computer work:

4 The teacher checks which mistakes were more difficult to discover.

5 Students exchange homework (preferably two or three recent pieces). They look through it all and try to find several typical mistakes.

NOTES

Error correction also occurs in the previous activity. We have deliberately given another type of error correction here because: (i) word-processors are available for all commonly used machines; and (ii) we believe it is very important for students to develop error correction strategies. There are many different ways of doing this. We have presented two of them. Students should be encouraged to build up their own individual list of their most common mistakes, adding to that list when receiving corrected work back, and using the list to check work before handing it in to the teacher.

Written work will increasingly be done using word-processors. Material for 'find the mistakes' exercises would thus already be in the computer, and once a teacher has learnt to transfer material from one file to another, a databank of students' errors can be created. This material can be used to build up a bank of 'find the mistakes' exercises, which can be made available to students in self-access. In our experience, students tend to prefer to do such work on text manipulation programs, such as total-deletion, gap-fill, multiple-choice, sequencing and matching-type programs, as these give students feedback on their decisions.

3 Schemes of work

Introduction

In the first two chapters we focused on the variety of program types which are available, and ways in which they can be used in individual lessons. However, lessons are not planned in isolation. They are closely linked to the syllabus for a language course and the aims of the general educational curriculum, and so should ideally be integrated into the series of tasks and activities which form the language course. If the main question we were trying to answer in Chapter 1 was, 'What range of software is available for use in the language classroom?', and in Chapter 2, 'How can the software be used in the language classroom?', the main question to be addressed in this chapter is: 'How can CALL be used as an integral element in a language course?'

In order to answer that question, we have organized this chapter into a number of 'schemes of work'. We present these as a series of case studies which show how:

1 CALL can be used alongside other media in a language course.

2 One type of software can be used over a period of time as the course develops.

3 A number of different types of software can be used for different purposes at different stages in the course.

4 CALL can be integrated into different types of language course, for different types of language learner.

5 The use of CALL can not only serve the existing syllabus, but suggest ways in which the availability of computers and software can lead to different types of syllabus.

We have chosen four case studies for our 'schemes of work'.

The first illustrates the use of one piece of software – a database – with students beginning English, and is linked to functional elements in the syllabus (exchanging personal information).

Our second case study is of students at intermediate level whose immediate purpose in learning English is to pass a public exam. The 'face validity' of the exercises they are doing is important to them. (In other words, they want the type of practice they do to resemble closely the type of questions they will be faced with in the exam.) The concern here, then, is not only with choosing software which provides the relevant exercise types, and with finding ways of using the software which will test the learners, but also ways which will help them to learn.

Our third case study presents a 'scheme of work' for advanced learners and shows how CALL can be used for a topic-based element of a syllabus. The topic is 'The Media', and the case study shows how computers can be used to investigate and write about the media (including computers).

Our last case study is a 'scheme of work' which has been used with university students on an English for Academic Purposes course. They are improving their command of the English language in order to go on to study English language and literature at university. In this case their syllabus can be considered to be skills-based, and the 'scheme of work' is intended to develop their skills of literary appreciation.

Each case study is organized into the following sections: focus, program and computer skills, methodology and finally, a list of activities. In Chapters 1 and 2 activities were outlined in full detail according to aim, level, time, preparation, etc. Here, the software used and procedure of each activity is outlined briefly, in order for there to be room for all the activities. Finally, each activity in Chapters 1 and 2 was given a number and title. In some of the case studies, there are a number of different, discrete activities, and in others there are more extended activities divided into a number of stages. Activities which are considered discrete activities, and not just a variation on another activity, are numbered and named in the same way as the Chapter 1 and 2 activities, to allow easy access to them from the list of activities and the cross-referenced appendices.

To summarize, the sections in this chapter are as follows:

Type of learner	Focus	Software used
1 Beginner – General English	The language of personal description	Database
2 Intermediate – General English	Preparation for an exam	Various
3 Advanced – General English	Topic – 'The Media'	Desktop Publishing Software
4 Advanced – English for Academic Purposes	Literary criticism	Word-processing

3.1 Databases for beginners

Case Study 1 — Getting to know you

In the early stages of most courses students learn how to exchange personal information in the target language. In addition to providing them with a means of finding out about their fellow students, this can have another 'survival' function, as they may well be called upon to provide this kind of information outside the classroom, either for informal or administrative purposes. We saw in Chapter 1, Activity 8, how, using a simple database, a file could be set up to store the names and telephone numbers of students. These were then sorted in alphabetical order so as to produce a class telephone directory. The same technique can be used to construct a larger file of personal information about a class. This scheme of work integrates the computer into the language syllabus by exploiting the fact that computers are particularly good at storing and manipulating information of this kind, and are commonly used for this purpose outside the classroom.

The activities provide opportunities for practice of a variety of language structures and functions, including:

(i)   'Wh-' questions — where, what, how;
(ii)   Numbers;
(iii)   Spelling.

Programs and computer skills

The activities are all based on the use of a database program. The teacher needs to know how to create a file and a record, and the computer skills the students need include:

Keyboard — (i)   Selection of capital and lower case letters;
         — (ii)   Use of Escape, Break, Enter/Return keys.

Database — (i)   Calling up a file from a database;
         — (ii)   Calling up individual records from a file;
         — (iii)   Moving between records;
         — (iv)   Moving between fields in records;
         — (v)   Opening up a new record;
         — (vi)   Entering information into individual fields.

In addition, for some activities, students will need to:

         — (vii)   Search for information in individual fields;
         — (viii)   Sort records on individual fields;
         — (ix)   Use the 'calculate' facility.

Methodology

The approach adopted in each of the activities involves students working in small groups, usually of three. While one student asks questions and the second answers, the third types the answers into the record on the computer.

If enough machines are available, the whole class can work in groups at the computers at the same time. However, some of the activities involve searching through updated records for all of the students in the class, and if groups are working simultaneously with different discs they will not be able to search for information about other members of the class until the updated records have all been combined on one class disc. If a network of computers is available this problem will not arise, as all the groups will be working with the same file. Otherwise there is some advantage in using just one computer with the class, with groups updating their own records while the rest of the class works on other activities. The disc with the file on it will then be progressively updated as each group enters information about themselves.

Activities

PREPARATION: 1

Before the first session the teacher prepares a 'personal information' record-format. In order to do this the language of personal information in the syllabus can be listed, and the items in that list used to set up the fields. Each of the different types of information will be a separate field in the record.

The following is an example of a Personal Information record, and the fields it might contain:

1 NAME 1 — FAMILY NAME:
2 NAME 2 — FIRST NAME(S):
3 ADDRESS 1 — STREET AND NUMBER:
4 ADDRESS 2 — DISTRICT:
5 ADDRESS 3 — TOWN:
6 TELEPHONE NUMBER:
7 DATE OF BIRTH:
8 NATIONALITY (OR PLACE OF BIRTH):
9 HEIGHT:
10 WEIGHT:
11 OCCUPATION:
12 HOBBIES:

The fields can be adapted to fit in with whatever syllabus or textbook is being used, with students adding information about themselves to the records in the file as they progress through the course. Note that the computer does not have to be used for each lesson, or for the whole of a lesson.

PREPARATION: 2   Before beginning the first activity it is worth considering whether any of the information stored in the records is likely to be sensitive. For example, would there be any objections to collecting and storing information about nationality? Would students be happy to talk about their height and weight? Are they happy to have addresses available for public access (even if only within the class)? To deal with any problems one of the following courses of action can be adopted:

(i)   The teacher can redesign the record to eliminate those fields;

(ii) Students can be asked what kind of information they would be unhappy about giving and having recorded about themselves. If necessary, this can be done by means of an anonymous questionnaire;

(iii) Students can choose to invent, or withhold some information.

N.B. This is Activity 8, which is fully explained on page 37.

FIELDS: 1 & 6   (Name and Telephone number).

LANGUAGE   (i)   Asking for names ('What's your name?') and telephone numbers ('What's your telephone number?');

(ii) The alphabet ('How do you spell it?');

(iii) Numbers 1–10;

(iv) 's as in 'What's John's telephone number?'.

COMPUTER   Sorting records into alphabetical order.

PROCEDURE   As detailed in chapter 1.

59 Where are you from?

FIELD: 8   (Nationality or place of birth).

LANGUAGE   (i)   Asking for information about someone's nationality ('What's your nationality?' or 'Where do you come from?'); or

(ii) Asking where someone was born ('Where were you born?').

COMPUTER   Using the 'search' facility in a database program.

PROCEDURE   This activity is carried out in two stages —

(i)   First of all, using the procedures described for Fields 1 and 6, students elicit from each other their nationalities and/or places of birth and enter them into the database.

(ii) When information about all of the students has been entered into the database, students then return to the computer in their groups and, using the 'search' facility, find out how many students of each nationality are in the class.

Alternatively, for monolingual classes, they can find out which cities, towns or villages they were born in. If students in the class are not only from the same country, but from the same town or city as well, the information could be about the part of the city they were born in, leading, for example, to statements such as 'six students in the class are from the north, three from the south, eight from the west and ten from the east of Athens' or 'six students were born in the 8th district, three in the 5th, and eight in the 12th'.

60 Happy birthday to you

FIELD: 7

(Date of birth).

LANGUAGE

(i) Asking for information about someone's age ('How old are you?'); or
(ii) Asking for information about someone's date of birth ('When were you born?').

COMPUTER

Using the 'sort' facility in a database program to sort a field into numerical order.

PROCEDURE

This activity is also divided into two stages, in the same way as Activity 59. During the first stage students work in groups to elicit the information about age and date of birth, which they then enter into the correct field in the record.

In the next stage students work in groups round the computer, sorting the records into order according to the date of birth of the students. They can then use the statistics they have obtained to prepare a chart showing the ages of students in the class, or to send each other birthday cards.

61 I speak your weight

FIELDS: 9 & 10

(Height and Weight).

(Before doing this activity care should be taken to check whether students are sensitive about their height or weight.)

LANGUAGE

(i) Asking for information about someone's height ('How tall are you?');
(ii) Metres and centimetres;
(iii) Numbers up to 100.

COMPUTER   Using the 'sort' facility in a database program to sort a field into numerical order, and calculate an average.

PROCEDURE   This activity is carried out in three stages —
(i)   In groups students enter information about their heights;
(ii)   Once the information for each student has been entered, the groups then work out the average height for their class using the 'calculate' facility in the program;
(iii)   As a follow-up activity students can then go to the library to try to find information which will allow them to check whether their height is typical of their age and nationality. A similar activity can be done for weight.

62 Future careers

FIELD: 11   (Occupation).

LANGUAGE
(i)   Asking for information about someone's profession ('What's your job', 'What do you do', 'I'm a(n) . . .'; 'I work as a . . .');
or
(ii)   Asking for information about the job they would like to do ('What do you want to do/be when you leave school?').

COMPUTER   Using the 'search' facility in a database program.

PROCEDURE
(i)   Students type in the occupations of their fellow students (or the jobs they would like to do);
(ii)   The most common (or most popular) occupations can then be found using the 'search' facility.

63 Hobbies

FIELD: 12   (Hobbies).

LANGUAGE   Asking for information about hobbies ('What do you like doing in your spare time?')

COMPUTER   Using the 'search' facility to discover similar interests.

PROCEDURE
(i)   In groups students type in each other's hobbies.
(ii)   The records are then searched to find out which students have the same interests, and which hobby is most popular in the class.

64 Testing testing

FIELDS

All fields.

At the end of term a similar activity can form the basis of an end of term fluency test.

LANGUAGE

All the language that students needed in order to complete the records in the file.

COMPUTER

Keyboard — (i) Selection of capital and lower case letters;
(ii) Use of Escape, Break, Enter/Return keys.

Database — (i) Calling up a file from a database;
(ii) Calling up individual records from a file;
(iii) Moving between records;
(iv) Moving between fields in records;
(v) Opening up a new record;
(vi) Entering information into individual fields.

PROCEDURE

In groups of three students sit at a computer with a blank personal information record. They then ask another student for the details needed to complete the form. A third student, seated at the computer itself, listens and types in the information. Students then change roles, so that they elicit, listen to and give personal information, and type it into the computer.

The activity is judged successful if a reasonably accurate record is produced. The teacher has to monitor the activity to make sure that the groups speak English while carrying out the procedure, and, if a group is having problems, tries to identify which of the participants has not managed to perform their part of the task.

FURTHER WORK

Databases in general, and this file in particular, can be further exploited in a number of ways.

1 *Adding more fields*: The record can be expanded by adding a number of other fields. Examples include:

13 Colour of hair:
14 Colour of eyes:
15 Number of brothers:
16 Number of sisters:

2 *Storing different information in the fields*: A parallel file can be opened which contains parallel fields, but this time the contents of the fields relate to the language required to elicit the information. In other words, Field 1 would contain the question forms 'What's your name?' or 'What is your name?' or 'What are you called?'. The database would then contain a file with information about the class, and another with information about question forms.

3 *Using the files for further language practice*: The information in the database can be used for practising other language items and language functions. The language of comparison is an obvious

example ('Six people in the group are more than x years old.').
Time prepositions are another ('Six people were born before 1975.';
'Ten people were born in February.').

4 *Expanding the audience*: The database can be used for joint work
with other classes, either by exchanging or by merging files for two
or more classes.

5 *Using other facilities in the database program*: More complex
searches of the database can be made. For example, searches can be
made on combinations of fields, such as height and weight to see if
there is a direct relationship. ('How many people who weigh more
than x kilos are less than y centimetres tall?'). The results of such a
search could be shown by using the facilities that some database
programs have for printing out graphs and histograms.

6 *Using the information for out-of-class activities*: It can be used to
set up clubs, by identifying the interests of students in one or more
classes. (It can also be used to influence the syllabus, since the
information about hobbies and interests can form the basis of a
choice of topics to be dealt with in the lessons.)

7 *Using the work to consider the wider implications of using
computers*: The questions that can be considered include:

(a) The kind of information which learners think should be kept on
    computers;
(b) Who should have access to that information;
(c) What use might be made of the information.

(The school should check whether there is a Data Protection Act in
their country of work. The school may be required to register the
fact that it is storing information about individuals.)

3.2 Exam training for inter-mediate students

Case study 2 — Testing time

Tests and exams are a feature of almost all courses, providing
feedback to both students and teachers on the effectiveness of their
work. Sometimes, however, preparing students for a particular
language exam is itself the main aim of the course, and this scheme
of work describes a series of activities with an intermediate class
who are in such a position.

We shall be looking at ways of using the computer to provide practice for the Reading Comprehension, Writing, and Grammar components. The exam itself is not computer-based, and, in the last analysis, paper-based examinations cannot be authentically replicated on the screen. Using a computer for additional practice does, however, have three advantages. Firstly, it provides an alternative approach – which students usually find more motivating – to a limited set of exercise types (which amounts to 'doing the old papers', and is often seen as dry by both teachers and students). Secondly, the self-access work it provides allows the teacher more time to work with individual students. And thirdly, freed from some of the work of correcting (and from waiting to have work corrected), the class can concentrate on the reasoning behind questions, and the reasons why students chose one answer rather than another. The practice is then aimed at developing language-learning and test-taking strategies, rather than simply repeating old papers.

It is assumed that the class is in an examination year which has 90–100 hours of English instruction, and that CALL could form 10% of the available class time.

Programs and computer skills

Whilst CALL software is often useful for language practice because it can encourage students to explore and experiment without evaluating what they do, the aim of testing is to evaluate rather than motivate or facilitate a student's performance. There is a limit to the kind of answer that a computer can mark automatically, since it is difficult to write 'rules' which will enable the computer to mark for grammatical accuracy, or to interpret meaning. For that reason the vast majority of testing programs are of the multiple-choice variety (or disguised multiple-choice, with the student typing in an answer, and the computer matching it up with a list of acceptable answers in its memory).

Since most paper-based tests also include questions which require open-ended answers, there are two ways in which computers can be used to prepare for an exam:

(i) Students take the test at the computer, and also have their answers automatically marked by the computer.
(ii) Students take the test at the computer, but just have their answers recorded, to be marked later by the teacher.

For the first type of practice we use partial-deletion and multiple-choice programs with our own authored material. (It is also possible to find programs of this kind which have been written specifically for a particular type of exam — such as the Cambridge First Certificate or Proficiency examinations.) For the second kind of practice we mainly use word-processing software.

Methodology

Our methodology in this scheme of work is influenced by two differences between language tests and ordinary language practice. The first is that tests usually involve individual rather than group work, and for that reason it is useful for students to spend at least some of the time working on their own on these practice tests. Some of the word-processing activities are interactive, however, and group discussions as a follow-up to the individual work are an important technique for helping students learn as much as possible from the activities.

The second difference is that tests are intended to evaluate what the student already knows rather than teach something new. Practice tests, however, are intended not only to evaluate, but to help students improve their performance when they take the real test. It is therefore important for students to realize that exam practice is not simply a question of getting marks for exercises which take the same form as the exam questions they will have to face. They should also be encouraged and trained to think about why they choose one answer to a question rather than another, why particular answers are correct or incorrect, and how they might improve their performance next time they do a similar test. In other words, the activities in this scheme of work concentrate on evaluating students' work, and helping them to get as much as possible from the evaluation.

A general point to note is that when mistakes are being discussed with a group or class, it is probably best to avoid identifying the student responsible for the mistake. Word-processing often helps in this respect, since text which is printed rather than handwritten can remain anonymous.

Activities

READING COMPREHENSION

A variety of techniques are available for testing reading comprehension but we shall concentrate on the most common, which are gap-filling tasks, or short answer questions. These can be either open-ended or multiple-choice, and the following examples illustrate each type.

65 Filling in the blanks

ACTIVITY

Cloze test.

PROCEDURE

Students work through a text in a partial-deletion program, but at the same time as trying to guess the correct answers, they note down the clues they use to choose their answers, and the words they choose, but which the computer rejects.

When they have worked through the test on their own, they then work in groups and compare notes. They make a list of words which the computer rejected, but which they think are acceptable. The teacher then checks their list with them and discusses how they chose their answers.

For each test and each gap a list of other acceptable words can be built up for the whole class. The word lists which each group produces can be compared, and new words added to the class list. In future, before the teacher checks a group's list, they can compare it first with a previously produced class list. This list could even be put into a database (see Chapter 1), with a field for each gap, and a record for each possible alternative.

This technique can also be used with multiple-choice programs. In that case, however, the students' task will be to decide why each of the choices is acceptable or unacceptable. In groups they then prepare explanations which can be consulted by other students when they do the practice tests in future. As with gap-fill tests, this information could be stored in a database, with each record representing a different test with a field for each answer, and the students' comments on the question.

66 Reading comprehension

ACTIVITY

Short answer test.

COMPUTER

Using a disguised multiple-choice program.

PROCEDURE

Whilst there are many programs available which offer either gapped practice with longer reading texts, or practice in giving open-ended answers to short questions, there are very few which offer practice with longer texts and short-answer questions. It is quite easy, however, to let students read a longer text on paper, and then answer the questions on the computer, using a disguised multiple-choice program.

Students read the text on paper, and then answer questions about the text on the computer. The teacher then asks them to make a note of the part of the text where they found their answers. When their answers have been corrected, they should be asked to try to explain why their incorrect answers are wrong.

In groups they then prepare explanations of the correct answers, and of the incorrect ones if there is time. These are then checked by the teacher, and typed into a word-processor or database file which can be consulted by other students who do the test in future.

COMPOSITION STAGE

The following activities relate to some of the more common text-types students have to produce in exams. The first activity is relevant to any text type.

67 Grading papers

ACTIVITY   Evaluation and Grading.

PROCEDURE   A file containing examples of compositions which received various grades in the examination is loaded into the computer. Students read them and discuss what grade they think the compositions would have got. They then compare their assessment with the actual grade. As a further exercise, they can discuss how the work could be improved upon, and produce an edited version.

This exercise is a typical exercise carried out by groups of teachers who are trying to standardize marking. This often leads to different opinions. This information could be made available to students in a file.

68 Recorded delivery

ACTIVITY   Formal and informal letters.

COMPUTER   Word-processing software.

PROCEDURE   Provide an example on disc of a letter which is a mixture of formal and informal English. Ask half the groups in the class to make the changes necessary to produce a formal letter, and the other half an informal letter.

Print out copies of the students' work, and discuss the differences with the class. Make a list of features which distinguish formal from informal letters. These will include salutations (e.g. 'Dear Sir', 'Dear Joe', 'Yours faithfully', 'All the best'), but will also include phrases (e.g. 'With reference to your letter', 'Thanks for writing'), and lexis (e.g. 'interesting', 'absolutely fantastic'). The list can be referred to during the next two activities.

ACTIVITY   Informal letters.

COMPUTER   Word-processing or Communications software.

PROCEDURE   Students can send letters to each other using the communications software mentioned on page 41. They can write to students in another class or to another school.

In order to evaluate the work which is being done, the teacher can check through the electronic mailboxes and note down language points to be taken up with the whole class. If the identities of the students are known, however, it is best not to reveal them. Alternatively, students can be asked to note down, say, three language points which they don't understand, or which they think are incorrect (again, without identifying the students from whose work these points are taken).

ACTIVITY	Formal letters.
COMPUTER	Word-processing or Communications software.
PROCEDURE	Students write letters of complaint to each other (e.g. about something they have bought, or a TV programme they have seen). They then write a letter of apology to the letter they receive.

Evaluation can be carried out as in the two previous activities.

Descriptive, narrative, and discursive writing
Activities for descriptive and narrative writing are described in Chapter 2, Activities 38–42. The main distinction which applies when using these activities for exam practice is the way the work is evaluated. For an examination class at a much higher level, one technique which can be adopted is to focus on spelling and grammar by requiring students to use a spelling checker. Students can then check the work themselves to find words which are spelt correctly, but are grammatically wrong (e.g. 'their' and 'there'), and words which the spelling checker considered incorrect, but which are, in fact, acceptable. Students can be awarded a point for each word they use which is acceptable but not recognized by the software.

69 Guide me

ACTIVITY	Guided compositions.
COMPUTER	Word-processing software.
PROCEDURE	Students load into the word-processor a file which contains the first sentence for each paragraph of their essay. They write a composition. They then print out a copy of what they have written, and put it on a table in the middle of the room. Students then take one of the other compositions on the table, compare it with their own, write comments on it, and return it to the table. They then take their own composition, which has been commented on by another student, and make use of the comments to produce an edited version.

A variation on this is to use compositions which have been edited by previous students. The first lines of each paragraph can be used as stimulus for the exercise, and students can then compare their own versions with the original.

70 The great paragraph divide

ACTIVITY   Discursive compositions.

COMPUTER   Word-processing software.

PROCEDURE   Students are given an essay to write on, 'The advantages and disadvantages of . . . '. Group 1 writes the introduction and conclusion. Group 2 then writes the body of the essay. The two are then merged and printed out. Students read the resulting essay and suggest improvements. The essay is then edited, and a final version printed out. The groups can then write another composition in the same way, but this time writing the other part. The edited compositions can then be compared.

ACTIVITY   Written speech.

COMPUTER   Conferencing software.

PROCEDURE   Activity 10, using a conference program, whereby EEC leaders have a conference at the computer – see page 42 – can be adapted to allow speeches to be written, and then broadcast over a Network. The work can be evaluated in the way suggested in the earlier activities in this section.

ACTIVITY   Grammar multiple-choice exercises.

COMPUTER   Using a multiple-choice program.

PROCEDURE   Students can work through a typical multiple-choice grammar exercise in the same way as for the Reading comprehension activities, noting down the reasons why they make a particular choice, and later working in groups to produce explanations of why choices are correct or incorrect.

71 Transformers

ACTIVITY   Sentence transformations.

COMPUTER   Gap-fill software which allows whole sentences to be gapped, and also allows alternative answers for each gap.

PROCEDURE   Students are given on paper a set of sentences to be transformed, for example, from the active to the passive voice, or from direct to indirect speech. Students transform the sentences and type their answers into the gaps. They receive feedback on their answer, then try and guess other answers for gaps which have more than one possible answer.

72 Dialogue completion

ACTIVITY — Open-ended grammar.

COMPUTER — Word-processing software.

PROCEDURE — Students are given word-processed files consisting of dialogues with parts blanked out. They complete the dialogues, and print out two copies. They then work in groups to produce a set of acceptable answers to each of the gaps. The teacher discusses the suggestions with the group, and prepares a file of acceptable responses, to be kept for future reference.

3.3 Media work for advanced students

Case study 3 — The medium is the message

At the intermediate or advanced level syllabuses are often topic-based, or have an important topic-based element, as this gives students the chance to practise language which they have learnt, and allow teachers to identify student areas of strength and weakness. This scheme of work is based on the topic of the media with the aim of producing a class newspaper, and is intended for advanced learners.

The range of grammar which is likely to be useful for this activity is enormous, but Reported Speech, Past Tense forms and ways of talking about the future are likely to be prominent. The range of vocabulary is potentially enormous as well, but vocabulary concerned with the media will be useful in talking about the task.

Reading and writing will be skills central to the activity, but other skills will be involved, especially if the activity is entirely carried out in English.

Programs and computer skills

The activities are based on three program-types, the most important of which is a Desk-Top Publishing (DTP) program. These programs are usually used with separate word-processing and graphics software: the text is written with the word-processing program and the illustrations prepared with a graphics program.

These are then arranged on the page by loading them into a DTP program and 'cutting and pasting' them. It is, however, quite possible to carry out the activities in this scheme of work with just word-processing, or word-processing and graphics software, though in that case the final cutting and pasting will have to be done by hand.

A Viewdata program is used in one of the activities.

The computer skills that are involved include:

(i)   Editing text with a word-processor;
(ii)   Preparing illustrations with a graphics program;
(iii)   Inserting text written on a word-processor into a Desktop Publishing Program;
(iv)   Arranging text in columns;
(v)   Using different fonts;
(vi)   Producing headlines;
(vii)   Inserting graphics prepared in a graphics program (or contained in the program library);
(viii) Cutting and pasting text and graphics;
(ix)   Printing the final document.

Methodology

Overall planning for the work includes deciding on the topics which will be dealt with in the newspaper, and deciding who will carry out the tasks. Each activity then has three stages:

1 Preparatory, non-computer, work on an aspect of the topic. For example, English newspapers are studied in order to produce 'rules' for writing headlines.

2 The preparation of text or graphics.

3 Integration of the text and graphics in the DTP program.

There are two main ways of organizing the activities. The first is to have different groups in the class working simultaneously on different sections in the newspaper. Their work is then put together to make up the finished newspaper. The alternative is to have the whole class work on the same section at the same time, each preparing a different contribution, for example, different letters to the editor. We suggest that you begin by adopting the first approach, and then continue with the second when the class gains confidence.

Activities

The following activities are divided into 'Pages' — in other words, each of them concentrates on the content that you might find on a different page in a newspaper or magazine. Before doing the activities it is worth taking your students through the warm-up exercises first.

WARM-UP

General media work.

PROCEDURE

Ask students to write down all the means by which they have in the last week:

(i)   given information to other people;
(ii) received information from other people.

Then ask them to think of as many other ways as possible that they have used in the past, and ways they know of but have never used.

Make a list of as many of these media as possible. They will probably include:

    (a) television
    (b) radio
    (c) film
    (d) telephone
    (e) letter

Compare differences in use amongst students in the class.

WARM-UP

Introduction to newspapers.

PROCEDURE

Bring to the class examples of as many English newspapers as possible.

Ask the class to analyse the newspapers from the following points of view:

(i)   Names, prices, circulation figures (if given);
(ii) Who they think the readers might be (in terms of financial income and political opinions);
(iii) The number of different sections in the newspapers, what their contents are, and what proportion of the newspaper is taken up by them.

In monolingual classes students can prepare a guide to newspapers in their own country. They can then compare the situation in their own country with that in England.

73 Hold the front page

Page 1—Main news

ACTIVITY

Main news stories and Headlines.

PROCEDURE

Stage 1:
In groups, students read two or three stories from a newspaper, each group taking a different newspaper. As a class they then discuss the style adopted by the journalists, and choose one or two newspapers to take as models.

Each group then takes a different story and prepares their own version in the style of the newspaper chosen as a model. The stories are then printed out and circulated for comparison and comment, and a final edited version produced.

Stage 2:
Students are given practice in decoding English headlines. This can be done in five stages. Firstly, the teacher can cut out some headlines and the newspaper stories they refer to. Students then try to match the stories and headlines. Secondly, they can be given just the headlines, and they write some notes to explain what kind of story they think the headlines refer to. Thirdly, they can be given just the stories, and asked to write their own headlines. If students experience difficulties these may be due to lack of knowledge about the events referred to, or they may be linguistic, so the activity can finish with an exercise in re-writing headlines conforming to the normal rules of English. Students can then produce a list of 'rules' for writing headlines. For example:

(a) Omit articles (Dog bites man);
(b) Use the present simple to refer to past events (Man bites dog);
(c) Use the infinitive with 'to' to express the future (Man to marry dog).

Once students have done this, they can then write headlines for the stories they wrote in Stage 1.

Stage 3:
In order to produce each of the pages in the newspaper, students will have to plan the layout for each of the pages. This is done by sketching the layout on the size of paper they are going to use for the newspaper.

If a DTP program is not going to be used for the Newspaper, students will have to print out each of the stories, cut them out, and organize them on the page. This may involve them in editing some of the stories, and printing them in a different format (for example, in a narrower column). They will also have to decide whether the headlines are going to be printed in a different size, and what design they are going to use for the title of the newspaper.

If a DTP program is going to be used, students will have to be shown how to:

(i)   Insert text written on a word-processor;
(ii) Arrange text in columns;
(iii) Use different fonts;
(iv) Write headlines across columns;
(v)   Cut and paste text.

This will be more time-consuming initially, but the results produced will be more professional.

For the rest of the newspaper a selection can be made from the following activities, depending on the time available, and the interests of students.

74 News summary

Page 2—International News

Students listen to a news broadcast (either live, such as the BBC World Service, or a tape made by other students, or the teacher) to extract news information. They can check their work by completing a summary stored in a total-deletion program. These summaries can then be used as the basis of news stories produced by the students themselves.

It can be useful here to use news broadcasts to revise the use of Present Perfect versus Past Simple tenses: the former often occur in the summary section of the news – where the news event itself is more important than the time of the event – whereas the past simple tends to be used when the details are given (e.g. Prime Minister X has been assassinated . . . It happened when she was . . .).

75 International news

Stage 1:

This activity uses three different programs at the same time: word-processing, communications, and viewdata software.

Divide the class into groups of at least six students. Two students will be at a computer using communications software, two at a computer with a word-processor loaded, and two at one computer where pages of information on a Viewdata program are displayed to students for short periods of time. Each group is given a different story to look out for and make notes on in the pages of information.

When they think they have the information, one of the students goes and tells it to the students in their group who are at the word-processing computer. Meanwhile the other student makes sure the information coming from the Viewdata pages is not changed.

Stage 2:

Students in each group connected to the communications program are given notes about different news items which they have to expand and broadcast to the other groups. The teacher asks them to send the information in small chunks, and gives them a time limit for the publication of their news page. Each group also has to take notes from some of the news items broadcast by the other group.

They should be told which news items to look out for. The word-processing group should be informed of these stories and then write them up.

The activity simulates the use of a telex machine in a newspaper office. Information is sent out and comes in, from around the world, and when information which students are interested in comes in, they have to pass it on to the team at the word-processor, who must write it up with a deadline for publication.

If you have a computer system which allows the computer to use more than one program at the same time, you could have messages coming in on one part of the screen, the viewdata information on another, and the rest of the screen could be taken up word-processing. In this case, the groups would be of three rather than six students.

Stage 3:

Students choose which of the items from the above activities should go into the International News page of their Newspaper and work out the layout as in Activity 73 on page 135.

76 What the critics say

Page 3—Reviews

PROCEDURE

Stage 1: *Book reviews*

Students write reviews of any novel they have read during the term. They can look at examples in English newspapers first to get some idea of the style and structure of a book review. If the book was borrowed from a library in the educational institution the location of the book rather than the price can be given in the review.

Students can also carry out a survey of books read during the term and produce a 'Top 5' chart. Comments made in activity 54 – on producing book reviews – can also be applied to this activity.

Stage 2: *Film reviews*

Students choose a review of a film or video and read it, deciding:
(i)   Whether the reviewer likes it;
(ii) Which aspects of the programme are focused on in the review;
(iii) Whether they think they will enjoy the programme.

They then watch the film or video, and in groups write their own reviews. Students read each other's reviews, and then discuss to what extent both their own reviews, and the original are factual, and to what extent they are subjective. This is a useful procedure to show students that published material contains both fact and opinion, and they must try to distinguish between them. The reviews can then be laid out, with some graphics concerning the film industry decorating the page.

77 What the editor says

Page 4—Editorials, cartoons and crosswords

PROCEDURE

Students read typical editorials in newspapers, and then produce one of their own for inclusion in their newspaper. The content can be about a national issue, or a topic of concern in their educational institution.

78 Cartoons

PROCEDURE

Students look at a sample of British cartoons and decide which they think are funny, which they don't understand, and which they understand, but don't think are funny. They can do this individually, and then compare their choices in pairs and groups, etc. If they are feeling ambitious, they can then try to write some captions of their own, or even produce their own cartoons. This could be done with a graphics program and then transferred to the DTP package.

79 Crossword time

PROCEDURE

Put students into two groups and give them a crossword based on vocabulary related to the media. There are two versions, each with half the words filled in, and these are distributed among the groups. Students then write clues for the words they have, using dictionaries if they wish. When they have finished they exchange their clues with a group who had a different version, and use the other group's clues to complete the crossword. (This activity is good for practising relative clauses.)

A blank version of the crossword can then be prepared with a graphics program and transferred to the DTP package, together with clues (prepared with a word-processor).

The material produced in Activities 77 to 79 can then be laid out on the page. Cartoons can be spread out on other pages as well.

80 Attitudes to TV

Page 5—Television

PROCEDURE

Divide students into groups and give them a different task related to discovering attitudes towards TV. (Vocabulary connected with TV, including current affairs, situation comedy, and soap operas, will be needed.) The tasks can include:

(i)   Finding out how popular different types of programs on TV are;

(ii)   Finding out which particular soap-opera characters are especially popular;

(iii) Finding out how much time students spend watching TV;

(iv)   Planning an extra TV channel, by finding out what kind of programs the class would like to see on the channel, and preparing a timetable to show a typical day's viewing;

(v)   Researching students' attitudes to TV, for example:
       — Is there too much violence?
       — Do people watch too much or too little?
       — Is Satellite TV of benefit?
       — Is video taking over?

The groups carry out the survey using a questionnaire and then write their reports. Charts and graphs can be used to summarize the results. An introduction to the page should then be written, and a layout planned for the material, which can then be put together using the DTP software.

81 A musical interlude

Page 6—Music

PROCEDURE

A series of activities related to music can be conducted, such as:

(i)   Producing a pop chart by finding out which records are currently popular amongst the class (or even going into other classes);

(ii)   Asking students to write about why they like a particular style of music;

(iii) Using the word-processor to write some lines from their favourite songs.

82 Letters to the editor

Page 7—Letters

PROCEDURE

Students write letters to the editor of the newspaper. As practice students can read examples from English newspapers first. The teacher can also select some topics from letters in the newspapers. Students can then write about these topics and compare their own letters with those on the same topic actually published in the newspapers.

83 The women's page

Page 8—Women

PROCEDURE

The class looks at examples of the women's page in a British magazine or newspaper. They then discuss why they think such pages exist and analyse the content and style as preparation for producing their own women's page. Male students working on this activity can be assigned roles by the female students.

One possible activity is for students to try to predict the new fashions for the coming season. They then draw sketches of the clothes and write descriptions of them. Another is to look at how the lives of female students in the class are different from their mothers' lives at the same age.

84 Financial report

Page 9—Financial Page

PROCEDURE

If students are teenagers, they can carry out a survey of the amount of pocket money or grant that students in the class receive and how they spend it. They can then write an article showing how expenditure and a grant or pocket money can be balanced.

Adults can carry out a short survey of stocks or shares, or other financial information, indicating which have risen recently, and predicting which are likely to rise in the future. If students know how to use a spreadsheet program, they can use this to analyse the data.

85 Situations wanted

Page 10—Advertisements

PROCEDURE

Students look at a variety of advertisements. They analyse the use of language, graphics and style of the advertisements, and discuss what makes a good advertisement. They then write advertisements of their own, for inclusion in the newspaper. The desktop publishing program may well have a database of icons which can be used in this process, or students could design their own graphics. In either case, knowledge of integrating text and graphics will be needed.

One possible item to advertise could be the students' English classes. The advertisements could also include job advertisements.

86 It's a goal!

Page 11—Sports page

Students write reports of important sporting events, either in their educational institution, or at a national or international level.

They can also write profiles of sports' stars (e.g. 'A day in the life of . . .'). League tables can be prepared (using a spreadsheet if students know how to use one), and icons similar to those used in important international sporting events, can be designed to put alongside the textual information.

1 Other pages can be added, depending on your syllabus, the interests of students and their language learning needs.

2 The emphasis of the newspaper can be changed from that of reporting events in the outside world to reporting only events of immediate relevance to the class or educational institution.

3.4 Literary criticism for pre-undergraduate students

Case Study 4 — Creative construction

Reading has been described as a 'psycholinguistic guessing game' and a process of 'creative construction', because texts don't have just one fixed meaning. Each person who reads the same text will interpret it slightly differently. An article about the British Royal Family, for example, can be interpreted as 'interesting' by one reader, as 'boring' by another, as 'critical' by yet another, depending on the experience, background, views, and also linguistic knowledge, of the particular reader. As we read, we are constantly constructing meanings and interpretations of what we have read, and of what we expect to read next in the text. One way of helping students to read and understand a text written by someone else is to give them practice in creating the same kind of text for themselves first, by writing on the same topic.

This scheme of work has two main purposes. The eventual aim is to help students analyse a fairly complex text. The immediate aim, however, is to help develop their editing skills by giving them practice in commenting critically on their own and other students' writing. Even advanced students may not take much notice of corrections made to written work, or comments made on it. Simply asking them to produce edited and corrected versions sometimes helps, but producing revised versions of written work is usually very time-consuming. Word-processors, however, make the task of editing much easier. Students can therefore be asked to produce edited versions of written work, and encouraged both to be more critical of their own work, and to be more willing to take note of other people's comments.

Programs and computer skills

The activities are based on the use of word-processing software, and concordancing software can be used in some activities if it is available. Some of the activities can also be usefully carried out using a network of computers.

Methodology

The work is carried out with groups of 4–5 students to a computer, and plenary discussion with the whole class.

87 Famous writers

PROCEDURE

Stage 1:
The teacher prepares a brief outline of the text that students are going to study. (They are not told what the text is.) This might be as brief as a one-sentence summary for each chapter of a novel, or longer if the teacher wants to ensure the inclusion of particular points.

In groups, students then expand the outline they have been given, using the word-processor.

Each group then prints out its own text, and photocopies should be made and distributed to the other students in the class.

Stage 2:
Each student then reads all of the texts which have been written, and prepares comments on both the language and the content. Each of the texts is then discussed with the whole class.

Stage 3:
Each group edits its own text on the word-processor, and produces a final version using the comments made about their drafts in the plenary discussion. They then print out their final version.

Stage 4:
The above three steps are repeated for each section of the outline that students have been given.

Stage 5:
Once the class have constructed their own versions of a text on a particular topic, they will have rehearsed many of the critical arguments which they will be able to put to use in studying other texts on the same topic. They are now ready to study the original English text on which the summary was based.

FURTHER WORK

Using a Network:

When students have had some practice with this type of activity, it can be done more rapidly using a network, as follows:

1 Each group is told under what name they should file their text. (Names of famous writers can be used.)

2 Each group is then told that, after writing their own text, they should look at texts from the other groups, and write comments on them. Instead of printing out copies of the text to make comments, however, each group can call up over the network the text written by any of the other groups, and read them on their own screen. Comments are then added to these texts, and saved to disc over the network. The group that originally wrote the text can then call up the comments and suggestions made by the other groups, and edit their work accordingly, before printing out a final version.

Using concordancing software:

If concordancing software (see Chapter 1) is available, students can use this to compare aspects of each other's texts. For example, there may be a number of phrases which some groups appear to overuse, even though they are linguistically acceptable (e.g. 'in my opinion'), or unacceptable phrases which are difficult to eradicate (e.g. 'according to me'). Using concordancing software searches can be made for these phrases and the occurrences printed out for discussion. Similar searches can be made on other items which are important for the text-type (conjunctions and organizers, for example).

This kind of activity can also be carried out without concordancing software, though the facility for printing out examples makes it much easier to see and discuss patterns of occurrences.

It is also possible (copyright permitting) to type into the word-processor some of the English text that is being studied. Comparisons can then be made not just with other students' texts, but with the original.

Acknowledgement
We are grateful to Charlie Farrell for this idea.

Conclusion

One of the dangers of producing a book with the title 'Computer-Assisted Language Learning' is that it may encourage the tendency to compartmentalize aspects of language teaching. We feel strongly that many of the areas which are now labelled as CALL will in the future be seen as standard classroom activities, just as the use of textbooks is not considered a separate branch of methodology with the label TALL. The focus on the machine will gradually disappear as more language teachers become familiar with this technology. Perhaps the best example of this to date has been word-processing. Many teachers turn naturally to word-processors for writing practice with their students, taking the hardware for granted and concentrating their attention on the pedagogical aspects of the activity.

Our main aim in this book, however, has not been to convince readers that they should use computers in their language classes, but to describe how teachers can use them without having to abandon their current methodologies and pedagogical knowledge. We do not feel it is necessary to convince teachers that they should use computers, since on one level they are simply another medium – like audio – and video-recorders, or overhead projectors. Teachers will use them if they are available, if they know how to, and if they see some value in doing so.

On another level, however, we feel it is unnecessary to convince people, since we feel that computers will inevitably become as common in the language classroom as they are with other subjects. This process will take time, particularly as, however much the price of micro-technology may fall, computers will still remain expensive in comparison with paper and books, and, even in the most affluent societies, education never seems to be adequately funded.

Microcomputers differ from other teaching aids in that they are not restricted to fulfilling one function. They can take over the functions of typing, printing, storing information, and calculating, and even transform them. Word-processing, for example, is not simply another form of typing. The ability to write, change, experiment, delete, restore, cut and paste, etc. before printing a final version, is potentially quite different from the process of writing in another medium.

Computers are capable of growing and developing and, if it is a mistake to label them 'artificially intelligent', it is nevertheless true that they can learn and be taught. What they are capable of doing is limited more by our own lack of knowledge than by their own inherent limitations.

In the short term, developments which are likely to be of significance for CALL include:

(i)   Standardization of operating systems: The most common operating system at the time of writing is MS/DOS. If a large number of educational institutions have equipment which understands this operating system there will be a wider market for MS/DOS educational software, which should lead to more software being developed. IBM desktop computers and their clones use this operating system. More powerful operating systems which are starting to appear also have 'hooks' in them which allow them to run MS/DOS software.

(ii) Linking of computers with other equipment: CD-ROMS (discs similar to the CD music discs) can store vast amounts of data. Dictionaries, encyclopaedias, and large collections of texts can be stored on one disc, and information accessed from them almost immediately. Videodiscs provide CALL with sound and vision, and, unlike videotape, allow almost instantaneous access to any part of the disc.

In the longer term, developments in artificial intelligence and natural language-processing will allow the computer to be used for more sophisticated assessment of language produced by users, and will allow more sophisticated exploration of language by learners.

For the moment, however, we hope that teachers have found the ideas in this book interesting, and that the activities we have described will have struck a methodological chord. The computer is, after all, just a tool, albeit a very powerful one, and we hope this book has helped you to become familiar with it as a tool, to the point where you can concentrate on the learning aspects of CALL without worrying about the technical aspects.

Appendices

Appendix A — Activities arranged according to program type

N.B. Where some activities use more than one program type, they are listed under each program-type heading. Please note that the activities are arranged in numerical order in the book and Chapter 1 is an introduction to each software type, in the order given below.

PROGRAM TYPE	ACTIVITY NUMBER
Gap-filling	1, 16, 44, 45, 65, 71
Multiple-choice	2, 24, 57, 66
Sequencing	3, 35, 50
Matching	4, 46, 47
Total-deletion	5, 19, 21, 40, 48, 74
Word-processing	6, 7, 25, 26, 33, 34, 37, 38, 39, 42, 49, 55, 56, 58, 67, 68, 69, 70, 72, 75, 76, 77, 79, 80, 82, 83, 85, 86
Database	8, 32, 36, 51, 59, 60, 61, 62, 63, 64
Desktop publishing/ Graphics	9, 28, 52, 73, 76, 77, 78, 79, 80, 81, 83, 84 85, 86
Communications	10, 18, 68, 75
Spreadsheets	11, 29, 30, 84, 86
Concordancer	13, 17, 22, 23, 87
Viewdata	12, 53, 54, 75
Adventure	14, 20, 31
Simulation	15, 27, 43

Appendix B — Activities arranged according to level

LEVEL	ACTIVITY NUMBER
Beginner	3, 8, 16, 25, 46, 59, 60, 61, 62, 63, 64
Elementary	1, 5, 6, 9, 12, 17, 18, 19, 31, 35, 36, 38, 39, 54
Intermediate	2, 10, 11, 13, 14, 15, 20, 21, 22, 23, 24, 27, 28, 29 32, 34, 37, 40, 41, 42, 43, 47, 49, 52, 65, 66, 67, 68, 69, 70, 71, 72
Advanced	4, 7, 10, 13, 15, 30, 33, 48, 49, 50, 54, 73, 74, 75, 76, 77, 78, 79, 80, 81, 82, 83, 84, 85, 86, 87
Any	44, 45, 51, 53, 55, 56, 57, 58

N.B. Activity 26 is an activity for both elementary and advanced students.

Appendix C

This appendix classifies the activities according to:

A Possibility of use with one computer
B Possibility of use in self-access, that is, without the presence of a teacher
C Degree of CALL experience needed.

Each activity is given a number from 1 to 4 for each category, with the following significance:

A Possibility of use with one computer:

1 with no adaptation
2 with little modification, for example, putting the students into groups and doing the activity as an inter-group activity
3 Possible, but with major modifications
4 Not possible.

N.B. See the notes on adapting activities to one computer at the start of Chapter 2.

B Possibility of use in self-access:

1 with no adaptation
2 the basic activity is possible, but without parts which involve the teacher or pair work
3 with major modifications
4 not possible.

C Degree of CALL knowledge needed:

1 suitable activity for a beginner
2 elementary knowledge
3 reasonable knowledge, for example, of authoring, or the more sophisticated features of programs such as word-processing
4 advanced knowledge, that is, complete familiarity with the program concerned.

It should be noted that the whole activity is being considered. If an activity has a rating of 2 for self-access or one computer, this normally indicates that the computer work is immediately adaptable, but that techniques such as group work will be necessary for other parts of the activity.

ACTIVITY	ONE COMPUTER	SELF-ACCESS	KNOWLEDGE
1 Verb Parts	2	2	1
2 It's all Greek to me	1	1	1
3 Question check	2	2	1
4 Toby or not toby	2	2	2
5 Invitations	2	2	1
6 Christopher	2	3	1
7 My weird neighbours	3	3	1
8 On the·line	1	2	1
9 Wanted!!!	2	2	2
10 EEC Summit	4	4	3
11 Journeys	2	3	2
12 Sports survey	2	2	2
13 Iffy	1	2	2
14 Treasure hunt	2	2	2
15 If I ruled the world	1	3	1
16 Question formation	1	2	1
17 Would you like some?	1	2	2
18 Test yourselves	4	4	3
19 Reconstruct the story	2	3	1
20 Presents for all	3	3	1
21 I am the greatest	2	2	1
22 Maybes	1	2	2
23 Finding passives	1	2	2
24 English connections	1	1	1
25 Recreate	1	3	1
26 Cross class interviews	3	3	1
27 Deep thought	2	2	2
28 Ideal partners	3	3	2
29 Fast food	2	2	2
30 Yes Minister	1	1	1
31 Reading about London	2	2	1
32 Censuses	2	2	3
33 Note-taking	2	2	1
34 Famous people	3	4	2
35 Dialogue reordering	2	3	2
36 Personal letters	2	2	4
37 Letters of application	3	3	2
38 Self-ish	2	2	1
39 Tourist guide	3	2	2
40 Passives and processes	2	3	1
41 Five in one story	3	2	1
42 The American tourist	3	3	3
43 Did the butler do it?	2	2	1
44 Sound me out	1	1	1
45 Spell·it write	1	1	1
46 Numbering	1	1	1
47 Negative prefixes	1	1	1
48 Translations	1	2	1
49 Sexist	2	2	2
50 A computer in the hand	2	3	2
51 Look what I've learnt	2	2	2

52 Shields	2	3	3
53 Personal News	1	1	2
54 Book reviews	1	1	2
55 Homework projects	1	1	1
56 Student worksheets	1	1	1
57 Find the mistakes	2	2	1
58 Correction strategies	1	2	1
59 Where are you from?	1	2	3
60 Happy birthday to you	1	2	3
61 I speak your weight	1	2	3
62 Future careers	1	2	3
63 Hobbies	1	2	3
64 Testing testing	4	4	3
65 Filling in the blanks	1	2	1
66 Reading comprehension	1	2	1
67 Grading papers	1	3	1
68 Recorded delivery	3	3	2
69 Guide me	3	3	2
70 The great paragraph divide	4	4	2
71 Transformers	1	1	1
72 Dialogue completion	1	2	1
73 Hold the front page	2	3	3
74 News summary	1	3	1
75 International news	4	4	4
76 What the critics say	2	2	2
77 What the editor says	2	2	2
78 Cartoons	3	2	3
79 Crossword time	3	2	4
80 Attitudes to TV	3	2	1
81 A musical interlude	2	2	1
82 Letters to the editor	2	1	1
83 The women's page	2	2	1
84 Financial report	3	2	3
85 Situations wanted	3	2	3
86 It's a goal!	2	2	3
87 Famous writers	3	3	2

Appendix D — Contacts

A Organizations

Information about CALL can be obtained from several different sources. Major international organizations such as IATEFL and TESOL have CALL Special Interest Groups and organizations such as the British Council also produce useful sources of information. Several addresses are also given which produce newsletters.

Teachers and students working in the state sector should check whether there is an educational computing group related to their subject area in their Ministry of Education. Alternatively, you may be working in a country which has a national TESOL or Language Teachers' Association, with a CALL Special Interest Group.

IATEFL (International Association of Teachers of English as a Foreign Language)

It has a Computer Assisted Language Learning Special Interest Group, open to members of IATEFL itself, producing a Newsletter called *MUESLI News*.

IATEFL
3 Kingsdown Chambers
Kingsdown Park
Tankerton
Whitstable
Kent CT5 2DJ
United Kingdom

TESOL (Teachers of English to Speakers of Other Languages)

It has a Computer Assisted Language Learning Interest Section, open to members of TESOL, which produces a *CALL Interest Section Newsletter*.

TESOL
Suite 205
1118 22nd Street, N.W.
Washington, DC 20037
USA

The British Council

The British Council has regional offices in most countries and the English Language Services Department have promoted CALL software and have produced specialist bibliographies of CALL literature and software.

The British Council
English Language Services Department
10 Spring Gardens
London SW1 2BN
United Kingdom

Other sources of information include:

ALBSU Unit (Adult Literacy and Basic Skills Unit)

This Unit is a source of information on the use of CALL in English as a Second Language and in Literacy in the United Kingdom.

Adult Literacy and Basic Skills Unit
Kingsbourne House
229/231 High Holborn
London WC1V 7DA

CALICO (Computer-Assisted Language Learning Instruction Consortium)

This is an international consortium which has an annual symposium in the USA and produces a quarterly journal.

CALICO
3078 JHKB, Brigham Young University
Provo, Utah 84062
USA

CILT (Centre for Information on Language Teaching)

This is the main source of information on the use of CALL in modern language teaching in the United Kingdom. They organize an annual CALL workshop and produce an annual CALL report.

Centre for Information on Language Teaching
Regent's College
Inner Circle
Regent's Park
London NW1 4NS

EUROCALL (European Computer-Assisted Language Learning Group)

This is a group of CALL practioners from a variety of European countries. They produce a newsletter called *RECALL*.

RECALL Newsletter
EUROCALL
Institute of English Language Education
Bailrigg
Lancaster University
Lancaster LA1 4YT
United Kingdom

NCCALL (National Centre for Computer-Assisted Language Learning)

This is the National Centre for CALL in the UK. It has links with many countries working in the field of CALL in both English and Modern Languages. It produces a sporadic newsletter named *CALLBOARD*.

National Centre for Computer-Assisted Language Learning
School of Language Studies
Ealing College of Higher Education
Grove House
1 The Grove
London W5 5DX

B Magazines and Journals

BYTE
McGraw-Hill Information Systems
McGraw-Hill House
Maidenhead, Berkshire SL6 2QL
United Kingdom

BYTE is the main monthly US computer magazine. It comes out in both an American and a European edition. It is a good source of information as to trends and developments in computer hardware and software. It can be rather intimidating for those new to computers (and those not so new!)

CALL Digest
International Council for Computers in Education
University of Oregon
1787 Agate Street
Eugene, OR 97403
USA

This comes out eight times a year and is practically orientated.

New Educational Computing
Priory Court, 30–32 Farringdon Lane
London EC1R 3AU

This is the main monthly magazine on educational computing developments in the United Kingdom.

SYSTEM (International Journal of Educational Technology and Language Learning Systems)
Pergamon Press, Headington Hill Hall
Oxford OX3 0BW
United Kingdom

This is the main Journal containing key articles on developments in CALL and other media.

C Software Addresses

Acornsoft
Cambridge Technopark,
645 Newmarket Road
Cambridge CB5 8PD
United Kingdom

Broderbund
17 Paul Drive
San Rafael
California 94903–2101
USA

CAL Software Project
Centre for Applied Linguistics
1118 22nd Street NW
Washington DC 20037
USA

Cambridge University Press
The Edinburgh Building
Shaftesbury Road
Cambridge CB2 2RU

Camsoft
10 Wheatfield Close
Maidenhead
Berks. SL6 3PS
United Kingdom

ESL Software Clearing House
201 Gordy Hall
Ohio University
Athens, OH 45701
USA

Heinemann Computers in Education
22 Bedford Square
London WC1B 3HH

Infocom Classic
125 Cambridge Park Drive
Cambridge MA 02140
USA

Longman ELT Software
Longman Group UK
Longman House
Burnt Mill, Harlow, Essex CM20 2JE
United Kingdom

Mindscape
3444 Dundee Road, Morthbrook
Illinois 60062
USA

Oxford University Press
English Language Teaching
Walton Street
Oxford OX2 6DP

Quicksoft
219 First N. 224
Seattle, WA 98109
USA

RDA Mind Builders
PO Box 848
Stony Brook, NY 11790
USA

Regents/ALA
Two Park Avenue
New York, NY 10016
USA

Scholastic software
730 B'way, 9th Floor
NYC 10003
USA

Springboard Software
7807 Creekridge Circle
Minneapolis
Minnesota 55435
USA

WIDA Software
2 Nicholas Gardens
London W5 5HY

Apart from the software which is available from regular publishers, many programs are also available on a shareware basis. Software can be bought in this way for a nominal fee: sometimes purchasers are invited to pay a further registration fee for updates and documentation if they like the software. The addresses of shareware distributors can be found in computer magazines: both the IATEFL and TESOL CALL Groups run their own shareware libraries and the ESL Software Clearing House at Ohio University, USA, is a useful clearing house for ESL shareware.

Appendix E — Buying Hardware

Buying computer hardware is similar in some ways to buying any
consumer durables. There is a wide choice from various
manufacturers. Frequently, the buyer also does not have the
knowledge to assess the various technical claims to superiority
which different manufacturers make. In addition, computer
hardware is a field which is constantly innovating. In this
Appendix, we can only give you a few pointers to look out for. In
order to place computer hardware in context, it is necessary to give
a brief outline of the history of personal computers.

Personal computers

In the late 1970s, developments in microprocessor technology
finally enabled the production of small personal computers. Early
machines included Sinclair's ZX80 and ZX81, the Apple II, the
Sinclair Spectrum, The Commodore Pet, then C64, the Atari 800
and Acorn's BBC B computer. These machines were 8-bit
machines, which is a reflection of the power of the microprocessor
inside of them. Apart from their attraction to computer enthusiasts,
these were to some extent machines in search of a use and a
common standard operating system. Their use was finally
established with the development of the use of programs such as
word-processing, spreadsheets, databases, etc.

Developments in microprocessors were followed by improvements
in floppy disc drives, that is, hard disc drives which have the
capacity to hold hundreds of floppy discs. Then followed printers,
with laser printers increasingly able to print publishable copy; and
screens, with colour graphics (CGA), followed by Enhanced
Graphics (EGA) and very advanced graphics (VGA) becoming more
and more widespread. At the same time, prices in all these areas
have been rapidly coming down.

Some of the early computers established a wide user base in
education. This was particularly true of the Apple II in the
American English world, and Acorn's BBC B in the British English
world, and to a lesser extent, the Commodore 64.

In the early 1980s IBM, who until then had been known as the
market leader in mini and mainframe computers, decided to enter
the personal computer market. It produced its own Personal
Computer, which was called the IBM PC. At first scorned, it was
improved and set the standard for Personal Computers in the
1980s. IBM also collaborated with a company called Microsoft, to
produce a disc operating system (DOS) which IBM call PC DOS
and which on other machines is called MS DOS. This became a
standard, and users got used to typing such things as copy a:*.* b:.
Other models of Personal Computer followed, namely the XT
(extra) and the AT (Advanced). These used more powerful chips
and had more disc storage. This range brought in the era of 16-bit
computers.

IBM's prices were high and this encouraged other manufacturers to make their own computers which were able to run MS DOS, and software written to run under MS DOS. These machines became known as IBM compatibles, or, more simply, clones. The net result was that it was possible to spend hundreds of pounds rather than a few thousand pounds in getting a basic IBM compatible.

Another development in the early 1980s was the introduction by Apple of its Macintosh computer. This was the first computer to deserve the label 'user-friendly'. It achieved this by what became known as a WIMP environment. WIMP stands for Windows, Icons, Mouse and Pull-Down Menus (or, according to some, Pointers). When making selections on a screen, the user moves a small device – a mouse – over a desktop, which then moves a pointer on a screen in between small drawings — or icons, which have a shaded background enclosed in lines — a window. These icons reflect their use, for example, a drawing package can be represented by an artist's palette; and pulling something into the rubbish bin in the corner, deletes it. Selection is made by clicking a button on the mouse. The Macintosh was also the first computer to be widely used for desktop publishing, using laser printers.

In the second half of the 1980s, IBM launched a new series of personal computers, called the PS/2 range. The higher models utilize yet more powerful chips (all the chips coming from a company called INTEL — the chips used being 80x8x, e.g. 8086, 80186, 80286, 80386, etc.). The machines continue to run MS DOS, but they now have the ability once associated with more powerful 32-bit mini-computers. In particular, they are genuinely able to do more than one thing at the same time — known as multi-tasking. The operating system which IBM and the Microsoft have been developing to exploit this power is called OS/2 (Operating System number 2). At the same time other operating systems such as UNIX (a popular operating system in the mini-computer world), or XENIX as it is known in the IBM world, are also vying for a slice of the cake. The WIMP environment pioneered by the Apple Macintosh looked set to remain.

Apple responded by bringing out an enhanced Macintosh, based on a more powerful chip (the Motorola 68020). Whilst the Macintosh has its own operating system, major software producers have increasingly been producing versions of their software which look the same when used on either a Macintosh or an IBM compatible.

Other manufacturers have also brought out products and created a large base of products. More and more IBM compatible manufacturers have appeared, with different countries having their own national products and brand names.

Finally, another trend at the end of the 1980s has been an increasing desire to link computers together into Local Area Networks (see Chapter 1), even computers of different kinds.

The important point of the above is that whilst computers are continually developing, at any one time there is a wide range of choice in terms of power, price and ease and flexibility of use. Some crucial questions that an educationalist should ask is:

Hardware components:

Computer — make sure you specify the exact model you want. Check what parts come with the computer (e.g. some computers are supplied without monitors).

Keyboard — if possible, try out different keyboards to determine which kind you prefer.

Monitor — there are an enormous variety. Check whether the monitor you are buying needs extra hardware putting inside the computer.

Mouse — can the machine support one?

Printers — there are a variety of printers. Make sure you get the correct cable(s) to link up to the computer(s) you are using.

1 What do I want a machine to do?

If the answer is: run the basic programs mentioned in this book, then a cheap IBM compatible clone will do.

If you have a larger budget and feel you have a need for machines which are nearer the state of the art, go for a machine which will offer you the more powerful ability to run more than one software program at the same time.

If you are planning on running a Network with a central computer, a file server, it is worth getting the fastest model possible within your budget.

2 What decisions do I need to make about the machine:

(a) Quality of screen presentation?
There is a range of models for monitors and the hardware that enables them to be used (or driven, to be more technical). Prices vary enormously from simple monochrome to state of the art colour systems. Try to see the images on screen yourself before buying. Check the lifetime of the machine.

(b) Monochrome or colour?
Again, perhaps finance will be the determining factor. Try to look at the software you wish to run in both set-ups, and then decide how important this is to you.

(c) Floppy discs or hard discs?
It is preferable to get a system with two floppy discs rather than one, if you do not have a hard disc. Make sure you specify the size and capacity of floppy discs you need. The cost of hard discs has fallen rapidly and unless budgets are really tight they make sense in an educational setting enabling material to be selected and loaded without fiddling with discs.

(d)　What kind of printer?

This depends on the size of your Institution. If on a basic budget, a dot matrix printer which has a fast-draft mode and reasonable near-letter quality printing modes is the best bet. Try to look at the model first. Go for models where the paper is easy to insert and change. This will save a lot of heartache in the staff room.

If your Institution produces a lot of its own materials, and/or plans to do a lot of desktop publishing with students, consider getting a laser printer. If this is work involving mainly text, a model nearer the bottom of the price range is satisfactory, but if you wish to produce material with sophisticated graphics, you will need a more expensive model which can support the Postscript language.

(e)　National or international keyboard?

It is possible with some computers to select the keyboard on the basis of language. Whilst it is possible to use software to enable a keyboard to type, for example, the diacritics of another European language, a particular keyboard can be purchased which does this.

3　Should I get a Network?

Individual circumstances will determine this, and you will need a member of staff with some computer knowledge. What we would suggest is that the machines you buy should be able to run on a Network *and* function as individual stand-alone machines. In this way, your hardware distribution is as flexible as possible.

4　Servicing?

It is important when buying hardware to buy from a place which offers quick and efficient servicing, including a replacement machine if a computer needs to be taken away to be repaired.

5　Is there a reasonable amount of software available for the machine?

Is the general applications software available of top quality? How much content specific software is available?

6　Other aspects?

Do not spend all your money to squeeze a much higher performance model out of your budget, and leave yourself with no money for software. Allocate the money for software at the planning stage. In the same way, budget for the cost of in-service training. It is much more important to get modest hardware, a solid starter base of software, and a well-organized training program than a room full of expensive machines which can show how quickly they can bounce a ball around on screen, but with no one actually using them in CALL.

Finally, if you are spending a lot of your Institute's money and really do feel in the dark, and there is no one to help you, consider finding someone knowledgeable about hardware and paying that person a consultancy fee. Even if this increases the cost by a few per cent, this is better than making serious mistakes over choice.

Appendix F — Software

In this section, we give some examples of software for each program type. In some cases the items are chosen because they are 'classics', for example, *Storyboard* is the standard total-deletion program. In other cases the item has been chosen because it is available on a variety of machines, and / or because it is easily obtainable.

Applications software, such as Word-Processors, Databases and Spreadsheets, is normally obtainable from computer stores who also sell hardware, or by mail order — look out for advertisements in general computer magazines. Your particular teaching situation will determine whether (to take word-processing as an example), you need a general word-processor, typically very powerful, or a word-processor which has been produced with a particular educational aim (e.g. to help younger students, or to provide word-processing facilities in a comprehensive range of foreign languages). General software is typically produced for the business world so is more expensive than educationally produced software. On the other hand, it tends to be extremely robust and more and more companies are offering substantial educational discounts. Major programs are also updated from time to time, so it is worth checking what the latest version of a program is.

We have deliberately been sparse in this section. Our aim is not to swamp you with hundreds of programs. If you are a member of either the IATEFL or TESOL CALL Groups (see Appendix D) and receive their Newsletter, or one of the other newsletters mentioned, you will be able to find out current information about the use and quality of current CALL software. In certain countries, teachers working in the state sector may have educational computing advisers, who can be consulted regarding the purchase of educational software.

Futhermore, we have deliberately not mentioned anything that is a wonderful program which A wrote, that B and C have a copy of, and that D has seen and written a glowing review of. Anything mentioned here should be easily available. We have also not mentioned publishers who specialize in software for one particular machine. Information on such software can often be obtained from the manufacturer of your computer. (Those specializing or targeting their machines towards education frequently have an educational software catalogue.) Furthermore, specialist magazines devoted to particular computers sometimes also have an educational section.

Finally, the larger publishers have now incorporated CALL software into their general distribution system. Specialist software houses such as WIDA in the United Kingdom are worth contacting for 'one stop shopping'. As an example, WIDA have a wide range of their own software for a variety of foreign languages and also sell European and American third party commercial and educational software.

'Authorable' indicates that teachers and students can write their own material as well as use the material which comes with the program. When ordering software, indicate the size of disc which you require (e.g. 5.25 or 3.5 inch.).

1 Gapfilling

GAPMASTER — WIDA (MS DOS, APPLE II, ACORN BBC) (English, French, German, Spanish and Italian versions). Authorable.

GAPKIT — CAMSOFT (MS DOS, ACORN BBC). Authorable.

2 Multiple-Choice

VARIETEXT — Cambridge University Press (MS DOS, Apple II, Acorn BBC) Authorable.

CHOICEMASTER
WIDA — (MS DOS, Apple II, ACORN BBC) (English, French, German, Spanish, Italian and Dutch versions). Authorable.

3 Sequencing

TEXT TANGLERS — RDA (MS DOS). This consists of a variety of programs including paragraph and sentence jumbling.

VOCAB — WIDA (MS DOS Acorn BBC) (English, French, German, Spanish and Italian versions). Authorable. This consists of a variety of programs for vocabulary learning, including word sequencing.

4 Matching

MATCHMASTER — WIDA (MS DOS Acorn BBC) (English, French, German, Spanish and Italian versions). Authorable.

MATCHIT — REGENTS/ALA (Apple II).

5 Total-deletion

STORYBOARD — WIDA (MS DOS, Apple II, Acorn BBC) (English, French, German, Spanish, Italian and Dutch versions). Authorable.

QUARTEXT

— LONGMAN (MS DOS Apple II, Acorn BBC). Authorable with separate Textloader program. This consists of four rebuilding programs.

6 Word-processing

There are many commercial and educational word-processing packages available for most computers.

WORD

— MICROSOFT CORP. (MS DOS MACintosh) A sophisticated word-processor. A version called WORD JUNIOR is much cheaper. Educational prices available.

WORD PERFECT

— WORD PERFECT CORP. (MS DOS) A sophisticated word-processor.

PC WRITE

— QUICKSOFT (MS DOS) Relatively cheap but sophisticated word-processor.

BANK STREET WRITER

— SCHOLASTIC (Apple II) Educational word-processor.

ABC

— ACORNSOFT (Acorn BBC) Educational word-processor particularly useful with young learners.

7 Databases

DBASE IV

— ASHTON TATE (MS DOS Macintosh) The standard in commercial databases, though with many rivals.

PARADOX

— BORLAND (MS DOS) Powerful commercial database. Considered by many to be easier to use and more flexible than DBASE.

RAPID RECALL

— RDA (MS DOS). Free form educational database.

WORDSTORE

— WIDA (MS DOS Acorn BBC) Educational database for storing vocabulary items.

PFS: FILE

— SCHOLASTIC (Apple II) Educational database.

8 Spreadsheets

LOTUS 1–2–3 — LOTUS DEVELOPMENT (MS DOS) Powerful commercial spreadsheet — the industry standard.

ABILITY PLUS — MIGENT (MS DOS) Integrated package including spreadsheet. Much cheaper than LOTUS 1–2–3h.

9 Communications

This software is of two kinds: that enabling machines connected by cables to talk to each other, and that enabling machines to talk down a telephone line using a modem.

Software for machines connected together in a Network comes with the purchase of a Local Area Network and information is best obtained from your hardware dealer. Two commonly used software packages are:

PROCOMM — DATASTORM TECHNOLOGIES (MS DOS) The standard communications program.

KERMIT — COLUMBIA UNIVERSITY, Kermit Distribution Center for Computing Activities, 612 West 115 Street, New York, NY 10025 USA. This software provides terminal emulation and file transfer for a variety of machines and operating systems. It is public domain software and distributed on a non-profit making basis.

10 Desktop publishing

PAGEMAKER — ALDUS (MS DOS Macintosh) Powerful commercial desktop publishing program.

VENTURA — XEROX (MS DOS). Another powerful commercial desktop publishing program.

NEWSMASTER — UNISON WORLD (MS DOS) (distributed by MGA MICROS, 140, High Street, Tenterden, Kent, United Kingdom). Low cost desktop publishing program.

| PFS: FIRST | — SCHOLASTIC (MS DOS). Another low cost desktop publishing program. |

11 Concordancing

| OXFORD CONCORDANCING PROJECT | — MICROCONCORD (MS DOS) Tim Johns (Oxford University Press, 1989). |

12 Viewdata

As with communications software, information on this is best obtained from hardware manufacturers, or hardware user groups, as the situation varies greatly from one computer to another.

13 Adventures

LONDON ADVENTURE	— CAMBRIDGE UNIVERSITY PRESS (MS DOS, Apple II, Acorn BBC).
THE HITCHHIKER'S GUIDE TO THE GALAXY	— INFOCOM (Apple II)
WHERE IN THE WORLD IS CARMEN SANDIEGO?	— BRODERBUND (MS DOS). A version for Europe is also available.

14 Simulations

FAST FOOD	— CAMBRIDGE UNIVERSITY PRESS (MS DOS Apple II, Acorn BBC).
AGENT USA	— SCHOLASTIC (MS DOS)
BUSINESS ADVANTAGE	— BRODERBUND (MS DOS)

Bibliography

Ahmad, K., Corbett, G., Rogers, M. and **Sussex, R.,** *Computers, Language Learning and Language Teaching* (Cambridge University Press, Cambridge, 1985).

Barlow, M., *Working with Computers: Computers Orientation for Foreign Students* (Athelstan Press, La Jolla, California, 1987).

Boden, M., *Artificial Intelligence and Natural Man* (Basic Books, New York, 1977).

Bongaerts, T., de Haan, P., Wekker, H. and **Lobbe, S.** (eds), *Computer Applications in Language Teaching* (Foris, Dordrecht, 1988).

British Council, *Computer-Assisted Language Learning: An Annotated Bibliography,* British Council Central Information Service ETIC Bibliography No 2. (British Council, London, 1988).

Brumfit, C. J., Phillips, M. and **Skehan, P.** (eds) *Computers in English Language Teaching: A view from the classroom,* ELT Documents 122 (Pergamon, Oxford, 1985).

Chandler, D. and **Marcus, S.** (eds), *Computers and Literacy* (Open University Press, Milton Keynes, 1985).

Charniak, E. and **McDermott, D.,** *An Introduction to Artificial Intelligence* (Addison-Wesley, Reading, Mass., 1985).

Daiute, C., *Writing and Computers* (Addison Wesley, Reading, Mass., 1985).

Garside, R., Leech, G. and **Sampson, G.** (eds), *The Computational Analysis of English*: a corpus-based approach (Longman, Harlow, 1987).

Grishman, R., *Computational Linguistics: An Introduction* (Cambridge University Press, Cambridge, 1986).

Hainline, D. (ed), *New Developments in Computer-Assisted Language Learning* (Croom Helm, London, 1986).

Higgins, J. and **Johns, T**, *Computers in Language Learning* (Collins, London, 1984).

Higgins, J., *Language Learners and Computers* (Longman, Harlow, 1988).

Jones, C. and **Fortescue, S.,** *Using Computers in the Language Classroom* (Longman, Harlow, 1987).

Jung, U., *An International Bibliography of Computer-Assisted Language Learning with Annotations in German* (Peter Lang, Frankfurt am Main, 1988).

Kenning, M. J. and **Kenning, M. M.,** *An Introduction to Computer-Assisted Language Learning* (Oxford University Press, Oxford, 1983).

Last, R., *Language Teaching and the Microcomputer* (Basil Blackwell, Oxford, 1984).

Leech, G. and **Candlin, C. N.** (eds), *Computers in English Language Teaching and Research* (Longman, Harlow, 1986).

Legenhausen, L. and **Wolff, D.** (eds), *Computer-Assisted Language Learning and Innovative EFL Methodology* (I & I, Universitat Augsburg, Augsburg, 1987).

Leonard, J., *Computers in Language and Literacy Work* (Adult Literacy Basic Skills Unit, Inner London Education Authority, London, 1985).

Leonard, J., *Word Processing and Language Skills* (Adult Literacy Basic Skills Unit, Inner London Education Authority, London, 1987).

Meyers, M., *The Language Machine: Using Computers to Teach Language Skills* (Taylor and Francis, Basingstoke, 1988).

Papert, S., *Mindstorms* (Harvester Press, Brighton, 1980).

Pennington, M. C. (ed.), *Teaching Languages with Computers: The State of the Art* (Athelstan Press, La Jolla, California, 1989).

Phillips, M., *Communicative Language Learning and the Microcomputer* (British Council, London, 1986).

Robinson, B., *Microcomputers and the Language Arts* (Open University Press, Milton Keynes, 1985).

Self, J., *Microcomputers in Education* (Harvester Press, Brighton, 1985).

Underwood, J., *Linguistics, Computers and the Language Teacher: A Communicative Approach* (Newbury House, Rowley, Mass., 1984).

Wace, G., *Never mind the technology, think of the information!* (Council for Educational Technology, London, 1986).

Winograd, T., *Language as a Cognitive Process, Vol. I: Syntax* (Addison Wesley, Reading, Mass., 1983).

Winograd, T. and **Flores F.**, *Understanding Computers and Cognition: A New Foundation for Design* (Addison-Wesley, Reading, Mass., 1986).

Wyatt, D. H., *Computers and ESL* (Harcourt Brace Jovanovich, Orlando, Florida, 1984).

Wyatt, D. H. (ed), *Computer-Assisted Language Instruction* (Pergamon, Oxford, 1984).

Zettersen, A., *New Technologies in Language Learning* (Pergamon, Oxford, 1986).